VICTORIAN PUBLISHERS' BOOK-BINDINGS
IN CLOTH AND LEATHER

for
HAROLD HUGO
in friendship and admiration

The Poetical Works of Cowper (detail)
Ed. R. A. Willmott
Routledge, 1858
Depth of design 102 mm

Blocking in gold on blue bead-grain
cloth, signed JL.
Collection Fianach Lawry

SUMMER TIME

IN THE

COUNTRY

ILLUSTRATED

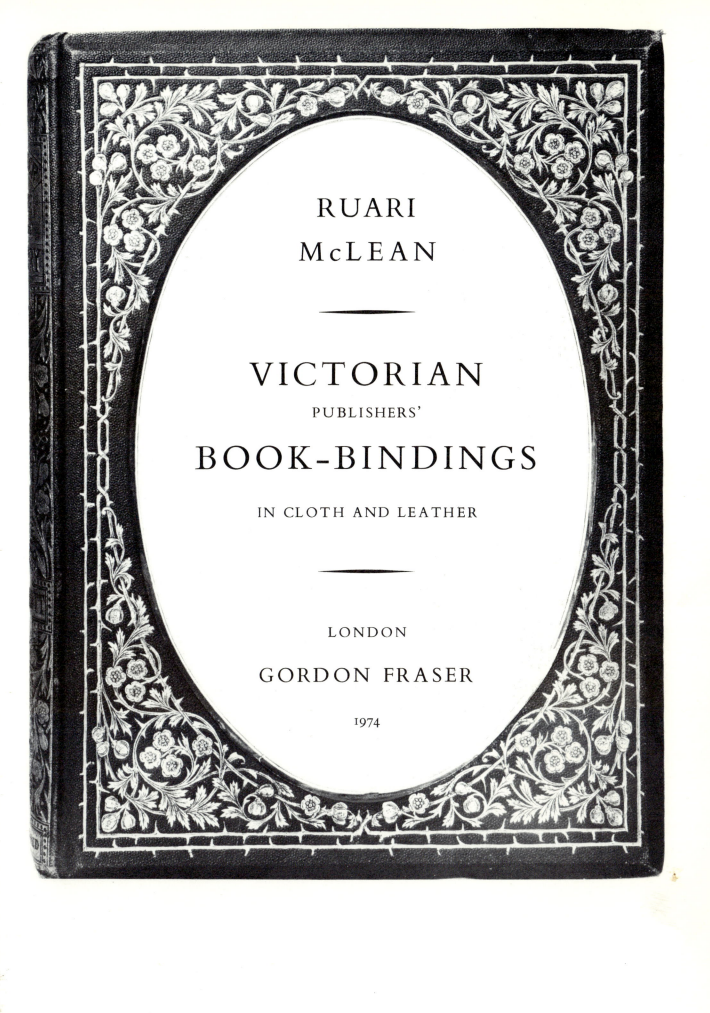

RUARI
McLEAN

VICTORIAN

PUBLISHERS'

BOOK-BINDINGS

IN CLOTH AND LEATHER

LONDON

GORDON FRASER

1974

The Gordon Fraser Gallery Limited
London and Bedford
First published 1974
© Ruari McLean 1974
ISBN 00900406 28 3
Set in Monotype Bembo
Printed in Great Britain by Lund Humphries Ltd, Bradford
Bound in Great Britain by B. F. Hardwick Ltd, Shipley

Summertime in the Country, 1858, shown on the title-page, is also shown on p.35.

λ9462

Steam blocking press, 1870s. From Annie Carey's *The History of a Book*, Cassell, Petter & Galpin, n.d.

Contents

The shifting sands . . .

We should be unwise, in the shifting artistic sands of our own period, in times when we face adjustments and adaptations as profound as those which the Victorians were called upon to make, to revert to the nineteenth century for complete artistic, critical, and philosophic guidance. But we may learn something from the problems they faced and the expedients they employed to meet them. There is something there for every taste. But the chief things are the richness, the inventiveness, and (in some instances) the daring of the designers of their books. They were people who studied eagerly and deeply the history of design as art historians, architects, and archaeologists presented it, who took the entire cultural heritage of the past as their own birthright, and struggled with the genie of mechanization to express themselves and their own time in the books they produced for their own use and delectation – and for ours.

It is a cluttered, serious, tense, calculating, sentimental, charming, and often amusing period. It has much in common with our own, a century later. Perhaps some of the answers for which we feverishly search can be found by studying it.

From 'Victorian Book Decoration', by Robert F. Metzdorf, *The Princeton University Library Chronicle*, Volume xxiv, No.2, Winter 1963. Mr Metzdorf's fine collection of Victorian bookbindings is in Princeton University Library.

Chess for Beginners, 3rd edn (detail)
William Lewis
Chapman & Hall, 1846
Depth of design 74 mm

Blocking in gold on green fine-ribbed cloth.
Collection Fianach Lawry

Bibliography

JOSEPH CUNDALL. *On Ornamental Art Applied to Ancient and Modern Bookbinding.* Society of Arts and Joseph Cundall, 1848.

JOHN HANNETT. *Bibliopegia; or Bookbinding.* 6th (last) edition. Simpkin, Marshall, 1865.

JOSEPH CUNDALL. *On Bookbindings, Ancient and Modern.* Bell, 1881.

GLEESON WHITE. 'Some Recent Cloth Bookbindings'. *Bookselling,* Christmas 1895.

BRANDER MATTHEWS. *Bookbindings, Old and New.* George Bell, 1896.

ESTHER WOOD & others. *Modern Book-Bindings and their Designers.* Winter Number of *The Studio,* 1899–1900.

M. SADLEIR. *The Evolution of Publishers' Binding Styles, 1770–1900.* Constable, 1930.

DOUGLAS COCKERELL. *Bookbinding, and the Care of Books.* Pitman, 1931.

JOHN CARTER. *Binding variants in English Publishing, 1820–1900.* Constable (1932).

JOHN CARTER. *Publisher's cloth, an outline history of publisher's binding in England, 1820–1900.* Constable, 1935.

DOUGLAS LEIGHTON. *Modern Bookbinding* (The Fifth Dent Memorial Lecture). Dent, 1935.

BASIL GRAY. *The English Print.* A. & C. Black, 1937.

PAUL MCPHARLIN. The Book on the Parlor Table. *The Dolphin,* No.4, Part 1, pages 48–54. Limited Editions Club, New York, 1940.

JOSEPH W. ROGERS. 'The Rise of American Edition Binding'. *Bookbinding in America.* Portland, Maine, 1941.

DOUGLAS LEIGHTON. 'Canvas and bookcloth'. *The Library,* 5th series, Volume 3, June 1948.

M. SADLEIR. *XIX Century Fiction.* Cambridge, 1951.

CHARLES RAMSDEN. *London Bookbinders 1780–1840.* Batsford, 1956.

L. S. DARLEY. *Bookbinding Then and Now.* Faber, 1959.

SYBILLE PANTAZZI. 'Four Designers of English Publishers' Bindings, 1850–1880, and their Signatures', *Papers of the Bibliographical Society of America,* Volume 55, second quarter. 1961.

JOHN P. HARTHAN. *Bookbindings.* H.M.S.O. for Victoria & Albert Museum, 1961.

SYBILLE PANTAZZI. 'John Leighton, 1822–1912'. *The Connoisseur.* April, 1963.

BERNARD C. MIDDLETON. *A History of English Craft Bookbinding Technique.* Hafner Publishing Co., 1963.

Bookbinding in Great Britain 16th–20th Century. Catalogue 893, Maggs Bros. Ltd. Spring, 1964.

HOWARD NIXON. *Bookbindings from the library of Jean Grolier.* British Museum, 1965.

GILES BARBER. 'Rossetti, Ricketts, and some English Publishers' Bindings of the Nineties'. *The Library,* 5th series, Volume 25, pages 314–30. 1970.

G. T. TANSELLE. 'The Bibliographical Description of Patterns', *Studies in Bibliography,* Volume 23. University of Virginia Press, 1970.

ELEANORE JAMIESON. *English Embossed Bindings 1825–1850.* Cambridge Bibliographical Society Monograph No.7. Cambridge University Press, 1972.

PHILIP GASKELL. *A New Introduction to Bibliography.* Oxford, 1972.

ALASTAIR GRIEVE. 'Rossetti's Applied Art Designs – 2. Book-Bindings'. *The Burlington Magazine,* No.839. February, 1973.

J. S. BUIST. Forthcoming article on Mauchline Ware in *The Connoisseur.*

The Cricket on the Hearth, 8th edn (detail)
Charles Dickens, ill. by Maclise, Doyle, Leech, Stanfield and Landseer
Bradbury & Evans, 1846
Depth of design 100 mm

Blocking in gold on red fine rib-grain cloth.
Collection Fianach Lawry

Introduction

This is a picture book showing the richness of publishers' bindings principally in cloth and leather, produced in Britain during the nineteenth century. Paper was also used, but decorated paper-bound books are so different that it is intended to devote a later volume to them.

The illustrations are mainly in chronological order. The only dating possible in a work of this kind is the date of publication as shown in the book itself; or, where it has no date printed, from the accession date of the copy in the British Museum when this can be ascertained. When neither of these dates is available, an inscription in a book at least shows that the book existed in that form at that date. It must be emphasized that the date of publication in a book does not *prove* that the binding is of the same date.

Publishers often bound only a proportion of the copies printed, and bound up the remaining sheets at intervals, according to demand, perhaps over a period of years. To complicate matters further, sometimes a very few remaining sets of sheets of an early edition would be bound in the boards of a later edition; and books also exist in experimental bindings, which were never officially published, or were specially bound as presentation copies. However, this is *not* a work of bibliography or a history of bookbinding, but a visual record of design in a most interesting period.

'Publishers' Bindings' means book covers manufactured in quantity, all identical, as opposed to hand-made bindings of single copies ordered individually and each a unique piece of craftsmanship.

Measurements are given in millimetres and show the outside measurements of the case. The width is taken to the hinge of the spine. Measurements have been made as accurately as possible, but book sizes, whether of cases or trimmed pages, vary for unpredictable reasons such as production accidents, and their importance is more to establish whether a book is large or small.

The colour of the cloth is given as accurately as I can, but some shades are difficult to define, especially when old, faded, or dirty. Many Victorian books are known to us with the same binding design but in two or three different coloured cloths: one assumes that they were bound in batches, and that when the second batch was bound, which might have been six months or more after the first, the original colour of cloth was no longer available. The publisher *may* have deliberately ordered, say, three hundred copies in red and three hundred in blue at the same time, although this seems less likely.

Nearly all Victorian book cloth was given a mechanical grain or pattern, by means of rollers, partly to disguise the threads and make the cloth look like leather, or, at least, something better than it was. My attempts to identify the grains are taken either from Sadleir's and Carter's photographs and classification reproduced in *The Book Collector*, Spring 1953, or from the photographs in Philip Gaskell's *A New Introduction to Bibliography*, 1972, themselves taken from G. T. Tanselle's important article on 'The Bibliographical Description of Patterns' in *Studies in Bibliography*, Vol. 23, 1970.

I have not noted 'all edges gilt' ('a.e.g.') because it is not strictly relevant to my subject, but nearly every book illustrated here does in fact have gold edges all round – one, indeed, (p.90), has alternate gold and red stripes, and that is noted. A very few were issued with 'gauffered' edges (i.e., decoration blocked or tooled on the gold edges), normally a luxury reserved for hand bindings only, and I hope I have noted all these.

This book has had to rely on extensive borrowings of copies from the collections of friends for photography. I am deeply indebted to the

Julia Maitland (detail)
Mary & Elizabeth Kirby
Griffith & Farran, 1857
Depth of design 107 mm

Blocking in gold on red morocco-grain cloth, signed JL.
Collection Fianach Lawry

The Owlet of Owlstone Edge, 4th edn (detail)
by the author of 'S. Antholin's', etc.
Joseph Masters, 1858
Depth of design 60 mm

Blocking in gold on green morocco-grain cloth.
Collection Fianach Lawry

An Anecdotal Memoir of . . . the Princess Royal of England, etc. (detail)
By a Lady
Houlston & Wright, 1858
Depth of design 75 mm

Blocking in gold on blue bead-grain cloth.
Collection Fianach Lawry

The Seasons
James Thomson
Tilt, 1836
107 × 66 mm

Red-brown hatch-grained cloth blocked in gold, identical design front and back, and on spine.
This is a very early example of gold blocking on cloth.
Collection R. de Beaumont

generosity of Robin de Beaumont, Christopher Dobson, Don Parkinson, John Porter, and Fianach Lawry in this respect. It is perhaps worth saying here that copies of Victorian publishers' bindings in fine condition are now extremely rare, particularly those in the more fragile materials like silk, velvet and paper; and they are least of all to be found in the great public collections such as the British Museum or the Victoria and Albert Museum Libraries, where for ages the original covers of books were thrown away in re-binding and repair, and only in recent years has it been acknowledged that the original physical cover of a book is also a document and possibly a work of art.

For unfailing courtesy and helpfulness in answering my frequent questions on technical matters, I am deeply grateful to Mr Howard Nixon of the British Museum, Mr John Porter and Mr Bernard Middleton. For most useful information on and identification of textiles used in nineteenth century bookbinding, I am grateful to Miss N. Rothstein and Mrs Barbara Morris of the Victoria and Albert Museum. I am indebted to Mr Stephen Moreton Prichard for his skill and patience in taking all the new photographs, in colour and black-and-white, required for this volume.

I. The techniques

DURING the nineteenth century the old methods of printing and publishing books, virtually unchanged since the invention of printing in the fifteenth century, changed radically: the modern world of mass production was being born. Books continued to be set up by hand, and were printed on hand-presses, throughout the century; but a steam-driven rotary press was used for printing *The Times* from 1814 – it enabled the newspaper-publisher to get his words on sale in the streets so much more quickly.

The way books were bound changed before their printing because a new class of book buyer appeared, in ever-increasing numbers. Before 1800, most people who bought books could afford to have them bound in leather, in a style of their own choosing, for their own libraries. Mr Howard Nixon, the leading authority on the history of bookbinding, described the situation in the following words: 'In 1810, the ordinary book was sold in stiffened paper wrappers or (sometimes printed) paper boards, with the edges of the leaves untrimmed. A paper label on the spine, bearing the author's name and the title of the book, tacitly acknowledged that some buyers of the book might keep it on their shelves in this state, but this "boards-and-label" style was essentially ephemeral: it had originally been conceived as a temporary covering for the sheets until they were suitably bound in full or half-leather at the expense of the owner of the volume.'[1]

It was William Pickering, in 1820 aged twenty-four and already the most design-conscious publisher in London, who realized that there were a growing number of customers for books who wanted something better than temporary paper boards, but who did not want the expense

[1] *The Regency Period*, The Connoisseur Period Guides, 1958, p.167.

and trouble of commissioning special bindings in leather. At that time, English printed textiles for furnishing and dress-making were probably the gayest in Europe, and an astonishing range of designs was available. Surviving sample books dating from the 1820s and 1830s (e.g. in the Victoria and Albert Museum) show stripes, floral, pictorial, and 'pop' designs at least as rich and attractive as anything on the market today; and incidentally, colour printing in five, six or more colours from wood-blocks on to cloth was being practised at least from the 1750s, sixty or seventy years before the same basic process was used by book printers.[2]

The first cloth used for binding an edition of a book (i.e. not just isolated copies, but a batch for sale) seems to have been a plain reddish calico, now usually found faded to an ochre shade. By 1825, the bookbinder Archibald Leighton[3] produced a dyed glazed calico which had the required quality of being impervious to the glue used for sticking it to the boards. The earliest book illustrated in the present work, *The Poetical Rhapsody* of 1826, is bound in a furnishing calico, with a design blocked on it in black: but decorated furnishing or dress materials were not much used for books, presumably because the cheaper ones were not sufficiently durable and the better qualities were too expensive. Bookbinders following the lead of Leighton quickly developed cloths specially adapted for covering books. The first form of decoration, which also served to camouflage the threads[4], was an embossed grain, worked on the cloth in the bindery either from rollers or from plates cut to the actual size of the book and stamped on to the cloth after it had been glued to the boards.

The most obvious finish to put on to book cloth was a grain imitating leather, and this was used in various forms for the whole century – and indeed is still used today. This was followed by fine lines, criss-crossed (diaper) lines, wavy lines, ripple and numerous other patterns, sometimes of considerable elaboration. Floral and other patterns were sometimes added to a block with a plain grain, e.g. *The Clan Maclean*, 1838 (p.26); when the design extends over the edges of the book's boards it shows that the patterned cloth was made in continuous lengths and could be used for books of any size. The next embellishment for bookcloth was of course gold – the traditional and most handsome way to decorate leather-bound books. Gold leaf is made to adhere to leather by pressure and heat; every letter, every unit of decoration, had to be put on by a separate heated tool, used with the utmost skill, taking time and, even in those days of cheap labour, costing money. To save money, binders could set up a word or words in a type holder and impress the line of type at one go: words so blocked can sometimes be distinguished by having a heavier impression at either end of the line, or by being slightly curved. Then, sometime perhaps as early as 1828, or at any rate by 1830, bookbinders – again it may have been Archibald Leighton – found a way of adapting an iron printing press to block a whole design in gold on to the sides and spine of a cloth-bound or leather-bound book. The design had to be forced on to the cloth by means of great pressure and, for gold, with heat; wood, which would have been easier to engrave, could not be used in this way and the designs had to be cut on brass.

For ordinary books, like novels, sermons, scientific and historical books, gold was used only for the title and publisher's name on the spine, with perhaps a small decoration on the front, but for gift books the decoration in gold soon covered the entire front, back and spine. The books so decorated, for long neglected, are now beginning to be recognized as among the most beautiful mass-produced objects of the

[2] See Florence Montgomery, *Printed Textiles*, Thames & Hudson, London 1970.
[3] Archibald Leighton (1784–1841), like Michael Faraday, was a Sandemanian, a sect that held that a man had no right to hold property. Neither man patented his inventions (D. Leighton, 'Canvas and Book Cloth', *The Library*, June 1948).
[4] See Bernard Middleton, *A History of English Craft Bookbinding Technique*, Hafner, 1963, p.133; and P. Gaskell, *A New Introduction to Bibliography*, Oxford, 1972, pp.235 ff.

The Boy's Spring Book (detail)
Thomas Miller
Chapman & Hall, 1847
Depth of design 95 mm

Blocking in gold on brown fine-ribbed cloth.
Collection Fianach Lawry

The Children's Picture-Book of the Sagacity of Animals (detail)
Sampson Low, 1862
Depth of design 96 mm

Blocking in gold on red bead-grain cloth.
Collection Fianach Lawry

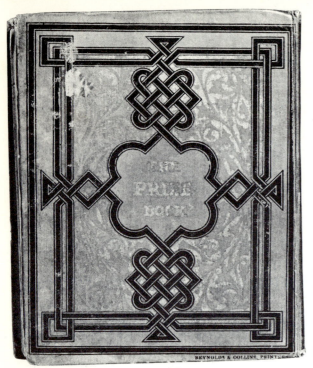

The Prize Book (detail)
Darton, n.d. (*c.*1849)
166 × 130 mm

Red-brown cloth printed in gold and
black, signed 'Reynolds & Collins,
Printers', identical design on front
and back.

Henry IV et Son Temps
M. L'Abbé Jousset
Alfred Marne et Fils, Tours, 1893
298 × 203 mm

Red cloth blocked in gold, silver,
blue and black.
Block signed A. SOUZE FILS DEL. INV.
SC.

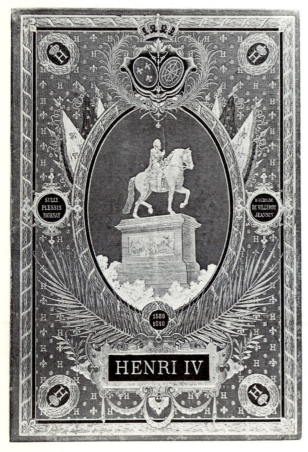

Victorian period and are the principal subject of the present work. Colour printing from wood blocks began to be practised commercially in the late 1830s. Gregory, Collins & Reynolds, founded in 1843 by three of George Baxter's apprentices, tried printing in colours on cloth as well as on paper (see pp.18, 37). This must have presented technical difficulties: it was difficult to print coloured inks on to cloth which did not get rubbed off in use. The number of books so treated seems to have been small until new techniques were developed late in the century. The decorative possibilities of using *paper*, printed in colours, for covering books were however, enormous, and were explored with such gusto for the entire century that they have been excluded from this volume with the intention of devoting a later volume entirely to the subject. Paper, usually coloured, was also used in the form of onlays on cloth bindings, and many examples of this kind of decoration are illustrated in the following pages.[5]

'Embossed bindings' are a variety of blind-stamped binding which became a fashion in the first half of the nineteenth century and which have been the subject of a recent Cambridge Bibliographical Society Monograph.[6] Blocking or embossing in blind on leather has been a regular part of the bookbinder's art from the thirteenth and fourteenth centuries; but the cutting of a brass or steel block for the whole side of a book and another for the spine, and the blocking (in blind) of a whole edition, seems to have started in England around 1825 and continued as a fashion for thirty years or so. It started on leather books, before cloth was being regularly used, and was used for prayer-books, Bibles and the Christmas gift-books and Albums fashionable in the mid-1820s.

The embossing seems to have been done in enormously strong iron fly-presses, in use before the introduction of the arming-press for blocking on cloth, and the pressure required was so great that the leather had to be embossed before being glued to the boards or fixed to the book. The process may have originated in techniques of embossing on paper which were being developed from about 1800; some of the Albums containing decoratively embossed paper, published between 1820 and 1830, are startlingly beautiful, and await a fuller description than they have yet received.

The designers of the embossing plates seem to have followed current leather bookbinding styles quite closely: a large number were in the 'cathedral' style, a part of the Gothic Revival, and were used principally on prayerbooks. Others were floral and abstract: some made use of engine-turned engraving techniques. A good range is illustrated in Mrs Jamieson's monograph mentioned above.

All the examples described in Mrs Jamieson's monograph are bound in leather, but the technique was also used for a short time on cloth. The only pictorial design (comparable to the 'cathedral' designs) that I have ever seen on cloth is the splendid ship design on some of Marryatt's novels, illustrated in *Victorian Book Design*, 1972, *XIX Century Fiction*, 1951, and elsewhere. According to Michael Sadleir this design was invented for the illustrated edition of Marryatt's novels published by Saunders & Otley in 1837, and was used subsequently on some earlier editions of Marryatt novels, dated between 1835 and 1837, of which the publisher must have had unsold copies in sheets. Although the use of highly elaborate blocks for blind embossing the entire cover gave way to blocking in gold, blind blocking as an ancillary to gold blocking survived for the whole century and much ingenious and attractive use was made of it. Another form of blind blocking was developed in the 1840s and continued in use for much longer. This was known as Leake's Patent 'Relievo leather' binding and was practised by the binding firm of Remnant and Edmonds amongst others. They were awarded a Prize Medal for them at the Great Exhibition in 1851.

[5]The word 'onlay' means material laid on to the basic material of the binding. The term inlay is used when a shape is cut out of the basic material of the binding and another material laid in the space provided.
[6]Eleanore Jamieson, *English Embossed Bindings 1825–50*. Cambridge University Press, 1972.

The following books were issued in this kind of binding:

	Binders labels
Gray's Elegy, illuminated by Owen Jones, Longman, 1846	R.&E.
Flowers and their Kindred Thoughts. Designs by Owen Jones, Longman, 1848	R.&E.
The Preacher, illuminated by Owen Jones, Longman 1849. Blocked in blind with same design as on wooden binding illustrated on p. 31	R.&E.
The Song of Songs. Illuminated by Owen Jones, Longman, 1849	R.&E.
Fruits from the Garden and Field, designs by Owen Jones, Longman, 1850	R.&E.
Winged Thoughts. Designs by Owen Jones, Longman, 1851	
Paradise and the Peri, illuminated by Owen Jones, Day & Son (1860)	Leighton, Son, & Hodge
The Psalms of David ('*The Victoria Psalter*'), illuminated by Owen Jones, Day & Son, 1861	
The Holy Bible. Binding designed by Owen Jones, Ward & Lock, 1862	

All these books were designed or illuminated by Owen Jones except the Bible, whose binding alone was designed by Jones and is illustrated on pp.98–9.

When it was desired to add colour to a cloth binding, this was usually done, during the 1850s, 1860s and even 1870s, by cut-out paper (or cloth, or even leather) onlays. An edition of *The Church's Floral Kalandar* illustrated in colour in *Victorian Book Design*, 2nd edn, pl.xvi, published by Day & Son, *c.*1869, has about thirty separate paper on-lays on its front cover. Another edition of the same book, illustrated in colour on p.126 of the present volume, has a totally different design, with red and blue pigment added to the cloth either by stencil or hand-printing, or both. *Pictures of Society Grave and Gay*, Sampson Low, 1866 (p.89) also has colour painted or stencilled on to the cloth, *not* printed or onlaid paper. The actual printing of colours on to cloth from wood blocks was practised by Gregory Collins & Reynolds, and possibly other printers, in the 1840s, but the method seems to have been soon discontinued, perhaps because the colours could not be printed with enough pressure and were found to rub off when the book was handled. The same objection applied to colour printing on to cloth by lithography, which was theoretically possible, and almost certainly practised experimentally, during the middle years of the century. There were also other objections – as Mr Darley points out: 'The lithoed cover entails double cutting up of cloth, much waste of make-ready material – and no work for blocking presses.'[7] Printing cloth book covers by lithography was never much practised in the nine-teenth century and for only a comparatively short period in the twentieth. The problems of blocking colours on to cloth are thus described by Mr Darley: 'The appearance of ink on the outside of books ten years after gold (i.e. *c.*1840) was due to an improvement in the design of the blocking press. The early presses had the bed of the machine fixed immediately below the platen to which the blocks were attached. There was, therefore, no easy way, short of detaching the platen plate, of getting an ink roller in contact with the blocks. The new press was fitted with a movable bed, set on grooved guides, which enabled it to slide forward, clear of the platen, so that inking the blocks became a simple business. Even so some thirty years passed before this cheap way of blocking was used as an enrichment of the then indispen-sable gold, and yet another twenty years passed before coloured inks began their rainbow progress which ended when the picture jacket forced an economic plainness on the binding case at the end of the First World War.'[7]

[7]L. S. Darley, *Bookbinding Then and Now*, 1959.

Three spines, for *Rustic Adornments*, 1856, JL, (p.63), *Country Walks of a Naturalist*, 1869, (p.133), and *Beautiful Butterflies*, 1871, (p.136)

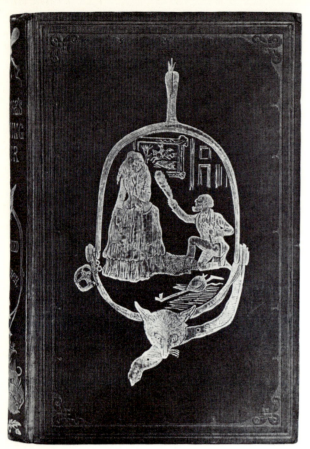

Mr Sponge's Sporting Tour
R. S. Surtees
Bradbury & Evans, 1860
230 × 143 mm

Gold blocking on red fine-ribbed
cloth, possibly by John Leech.
Collection Fianach Lawry

Snow-Flakes
M. Betham-Edwards
Sampson Low, n.d. (1862?)
190 × 140 mm

Gold blocking on green cloth.
Collection Fianach Lawry

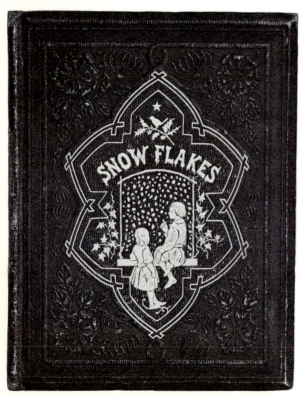

Colour blocking on cloth began to be used in England more during the 1870s, when design was at its lowest, and was much used for children's books during the 1880s. A series of well designed cloth covers blocked in four or more colours was produced at the turn of the century by Ernest Nister, e.g. *Robinson Crusoe*, n.d. (p.144), *Life's Roses*, n.d. (inscribed 1898) (see p.158), Lamb's *Tales from Shakespeare*, n.d. (inscribed 1903), and *The Vicar of Wakefield*, n.d. (inscribed 1906); all of these seem to have been printed and bound in Bavaria. A much more elaborate style of colour blocking on cloth became characteristic of gift book publishing in France towards the close of the century. Probably the best-known are those on Hetzel's collected edition of Jules Verne, some of which were blocked in gold and up to six colours (c.f. *Victorian Book Design*, 2nd edn, p.225), but there were many others, of great richness, using silver and gold as well as colours. Perhaps the finest pictorial colour-blocked bindings ever made were the series of children's books on the history of France, illustrated by Job, Maurice Leloir and others, published in Paris by Boivin, in the years immediately preceding the First World War.

As a footnote to the history of gold blocking on cloth, it may be mentioned here that the elaborate hand-engraved brass plates must have represented a considerable investment for publishers, and were not infrequently re-used (where the title was not an integral part of the design, or could be cut out) for a later and completely different book. Sometimes, if the later book was smaller, the brass was cut down; a border, for example, could be shortened by cutting out a section of it. Two books with the same cover block are shown on pp.116–7.

Besides cloth and leather, other materials used for publishers' bindings during the nineteenth century illustrated in these pages include wood (pp.31, 48–9), imitation tortoise-shell (p.109) and malachite (p.106). One publisher, Paul Jerrard, who specialized in 'elegant Drawing-Room Books' and 'Cream and Gold special presents', advertised at least one book as being bound in porcelain; but I suspect that this may in fact have been a highly varnished papier mâché. The black papier mâché bindings imitating ebony, used on the illuminated and other books by Owen Jones and Henry Noel Humphreys, will be illustrated in our second volume dealing with books bound in paper and paper boards.

II. The designs

At the beginning of the nineteenth century, the general appearance of a book was dictated by the publisher, who was paying for it. The typographic design was normally left to the printer. In England, at the beginning of the nineteenth century, there were at least three printers with an outstanding sense of typographic style, Bulmer, Bensley, and Charles Whittingham the elder. Most other printers, up and down the country, could set up a plain title-page with restraint and dignity.

But the profession of publishing was beginning to take its modern shape: men were emerging who commissioned books to meet commercial needs which they could see, and who, having created the contents, gave thought also to their appearance. One of the first of these was Rudolph Ackermann (1764–1834), whose *Forget Me Not* annuals, starting in 1825, were among the earliest English books deliberately packaged as gifts – bound in gay paper, later in watered silk, (see p.20) encased in extremely pretty decorated cartons – a style which originated on the Continent.

William Pickering (1796–1854) was another publisher who cared very much what his books looked like. Pickering did not, to any great extent, go in for the Christmas gift book and annual trade, for which the more elaborately designed books shown in these pages were destined. He went in mostly for poetry, historical and theological reprints, and general literature: in the series of folio reprints of historic editions of the Book of Common Prayer, printed at the Chiswick Press, which he published in 1844, bound in parchment gilt, he produced the crowning achievement of his collaboration with the Whittinghams, and a typographical monument to his age. It was Pickering who first suggested to his binder the use of cloth for binding editions, and thereby revolutionized the appearance of books for a century or more; but Pickering's books rarely carried the elaborate gold-blocked decoration soon favoured by other publishers. He favoured plain cloth, usually with paper labels on the spines, but sometimes with the titles plainly blocked in gold, with or without a plain rule round them. One of his rare octavo books with coloured plates, Louisa Stuart Costello's *Specimens of the Early Poetry of France*, 1835, appeared in brown morocco-grained cloth with an elaborate blind-stamped decoration centred on front and back – a subtle and distinguished binding, but sober in comparison with others of its day. The works of Henry Shaw published by Pickering, which were mostly large volumes, beautifully printed by the Chiswick Press with coloured illustrations, were issued in a very plain style, half leather or cloth with plain red paper sides. These were books for which many owners commissioned special bindings in leather. A twenty-page catalogue of Pickering's publications, dated October 1848, hardly mentions bindings at all. There is only one mention of the word 'cloth' ('Aldine Edition of the Poets, price 5s. each volume in cloth boards, or 10s. 6d. bound in morocco by Hayday') in the entire catalogue, because by that date it had become the normal material in which Pickering's books were issued.

Several other smaller publishers of the period, notably D. A. Talboys and Francis Macpherson, both of Oxford, adopted Pickering's binding style of self-effacing smooth cloth with paper labels at the tops of the spines: their books, inside and out, were distinguished and are still today a joy to handle.

Joseph Cundall (1818–95), another design-conscious publisher, did produce books for the gift book market, and for children. He was particularly interested in decorative bindings, commissioned many, lectured on them to the Royal Society of Arts, and late in life wrote a history of bookbinding (which as usual more or less ignored his own period). Several books which must have been designed to his specification or suggestions are illustrated here. Many of his children's books, e.g. the Home Treasury and Gammer Gurton series, were issued in beautiful colour-printed paper covers with designs after Holbein or Raphael – ideas which may have come from Cundall, but perhaps more probably from Henry Cole, the originator and editor of the series.

Before 1850, most designs on publisher's bindings are unsigned. If a book is illustrated, it is tempting to guess that the illustrator would also have been asked to make a design for the binding, but there are so many cases when this clearly did not happen that such assumption can rarely be relied on. But gradually, professional designers of publisher's bindings emerge. The earliest binding designs so far identified by signatures are on two books dated 1845, Eugène Sue's *Paula Monti*, Chapman & Hall, and Camilla Toulmin's *Lays and Legends Illustrative of English Life*, Howe, both signed JL, for John Leighton (1822–1912). John Leighton, who also used the pseudonym Luke Limner, 'was, even for a Victorian of the generation of Owen Jones and Matthew Digby

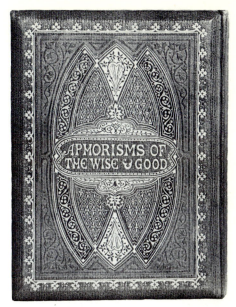

Aphorisms of the Wise and Good
Illum. S. Stanesby
Griffith & Farran, n.d. (c.1860)
145 × 105 mm

Green cloth blocked in blind and gold on red and purple paper onlays on front and back, spine blocked in gold only, bevelled boards.
Bound by Hanbury & Co., Binders, 80 Coleman Street, EC.
Collection Fianach Lawry

The Triumphs of Perseverance and Enterprise
Darton & Co., n.d. (c.1860)
185 × 120 mm

Red wavy patterned cloth blocked in gold on front and spine, in blind on back.
Collection Christopher Dobson

The Eve of St Agnes (detail)
John Keats
Sampson Low for Joseph Cundall,
   1856
Depth of design 100 mm

Blocking in gold on purple morocco-
grain cloth, signed JL.
Collection Fianach Lawry

Poets' Wit & Humour
Bell & Daldy, 1861
235 × 168 mm

Blocked in gold and blind on red
cloth on front and spine, with
diamond shaped blue paper onlay on
front blocked in gold, Signed R.D.

Wyatt, an exceptionally active and verstile commercial artist.'[8] One thinks of him also as one of the earliest 'designers' (as opposed to 'artists', although the distinction did not exist to the Victorians) of the nineteenth century, He wrote and illustrated books, designed bank notes, Christmas cards, monograms, magazine covers, stained glass, monuments, Albert Memorial Tazza in ceramic ware and a 'luminous fireplace', but his designs for publisher's bindings in cloth were probably his most continuing employment and are his most lasting memorial. A study of his complete work is badly needed: here it can only be said that his designs were original and never pastiche, were endlessly inventive, witty, amazingly unrepetitive and admirably professional. Miss Pantazzi, in the article cited above, points out that Leighton was a follower of Owen Jones's dicta that in applied design, natural forms must be flat and conventional: three-dimensional effects were not allowed. (He did *not* follow the government officer in *Hard Times* (1854) who said 'You are to be in all things regulated and governed by fact . . . You must discard the word Fancy altogether. You have nothing to do with it. You are not to have, in any object of use or ornament, what would be a contradiction in fact. You don't walk upon flowers in fact; you cannot be allowed to walk upon flowers in carpets. You don't find that foreign birds and butterflies come and perch upon your crockery; you cannot be permitted to paint foreign birds and butterflies upon your crockery.')

Miss Pantazzi points out that Leighton rarely made use of the diaper or repeating pattern which is a most effective device in bookbinding design. 'He evolved', she says, 'a style of his own which at its best is recognizable by the marvellous delicacy of its detail and by its individual and endearing combination of every variety of Victorian ornament.' A problem, in considering his work, is that he certainly did not sign everything he did (one longs to know on what basis he signed, or didn't) and there is a large number of binding designs one wants to, but cannot, attribute to him with certainty. What is particularly tantalizing is that several of the finest designs of the whole period are unsigned, and must continue to glow with anonymous distinction until someone can find evidence which will identify them.

The three most prolific designers of book covers after Leighton are William Harry Rogers (1825–1873) who signed WHR and WR, (the earliest gold-blocked cloth binding signed WHR may be *Excelsior*, by 'Alastor', published by Pickering in 1852, see p.46), Albert Henry Warren (1830–1911) who signed AW or W, and Robert Dudley, active 1858–1891, who signed RD. Several examples of these artists' work are illustrated here. Other identified designers are John Sliegh (JS or S,) Thomas Robert Macquoid (TM and TRM), Thomas Sulman, Owen Jones (who rarely signed, but is generally credited inside the book) and Matthew Digby Wyatt. In addition, bindings exist with various as yet unidentified initials, such as JM, CB, and combinations of C and T, J and M, and C and H.

Many would say that the greatest period of Victorian gift book design was the sixties, the climax of monochrome wood-engraved illustration, when such books were actually planned and commissioned by the great wood-engraving firms of Dalziel, Swain, and Evans. This was also the culmination of the gold-blocked cloth binding: after the sixties, the quality of design at first gradually, then swiftly, deteriorated.

Abstract design and decoration during the seventies lost all purpose and meaning: its dreariness was emphasized by a growing use of black ink instead of gold. But, while abstract decoration became more and more futile, illustration began to be used increasingly on cloth book covers, blocked in coloured inks, and some effective and amusing designs were produced in this way.

While the general level of design clearly lacked inspiration, a revival was on its way, illustrated on the last seven pages of this book. First,

[8]Sybille Pantazzi, 'John Leighton, 1822–1912', *The Connoisseur*, April 1963, pp.262–273.

there were Dante Gabriel Rossetti's remarkable designs, of which the earliest was probably *The Early Italian Poets*, 1861. Three others of his are shown on pp.152–3, utterly different from anything else of their own day. The linear design on *Goblin Market* (of all titles) looks forward to Mondrian. Then, during the seventies and eighties, there were excellent designs on cloth by Caldecott and Crane, followed by a succession of marvellous covers, all blocked in gold on dark blue cloth, published mostly by Macmillan, right through the nineties. Some of these covers harked back to the great tradition of the forties and fifties, but others revealed new ideas of art nouveau and the twentieth century to come. The superb cover designs made by Gordon Craig, Charles Ricketts, Laurence Housman, Beardsley, Crawhall, Nicholson, Joseph Simpson, and others, all before 1900, are part of the modern world of today.

III. Contemporary criticism

I HAVE been able to find very few contemporary accounts or criticisms of the prolific and, one would have thought, conspicuous activity of design illustrated in these pages.

The earliest is a paper read by Joseph Cundall, the publisher, to a meeting of the Society of Arts in November 1847, and published in 1848 as *On Ornamental Art, applied to ancient and modern bookbinding*, by the Society of Arts and Joseph Cundall at 12 Old Bond Street. It is a handsome quarto, printed by the Chiswick Press, and is invaluable in that it actually illustrates three contemporary English publishers' cloth binding designs.

Cundall criticized Owen Jones, who was probably in the audience, in the following passage: 'To Mr Owen Jones we are indebted for several ornamental designs in embossed leather; but, from the peculiar treatment which that gentleman has given them, some few are more beautiful than appropriate. For instance, *Gray's Elegy*, one of the finest and most *English* of English poems, appeared, dressed internally and externally in an old-fashioned, monkish garb [i.e. the text was illuminated like a medieval manuscript, and the binding was in relievo leather]. The bindings of the *Floral Albums*, and *Flowers and their Kindred Thoughts* [see p.32] are more suitable, and the embossed covers of *Murray's Prayer-book* and the little *Prayer-books* show that we have advanced in the right path; remembering, as we do, the great church windows and gothic doorways which used to be perpetrated on our bibles [i.e. the now admired 'cathedral' bindings, see p.21].'

He then criticized his friend and patron Henry Cole, saying 'Mr Felix Summerly [Henry Cole] was one of the first to give us adaptations of old patterns on the bindings of books; but I think it may be questioned whether Grolier patterns of the sixteenth century are very appropriate to modern guide books.' (Cundall himself had published modern children's books with Grolier-pattern bindings, see p.18).

He finally makes two very constructive and valid points: first, 'every book should be decorated as far as possible in accordance with its contents'; and secondly, a plea for original contemporary design, not historical copying: 'Let us hope then, that it will not be long ere such original ornamental art shall be wedded to our present perfect

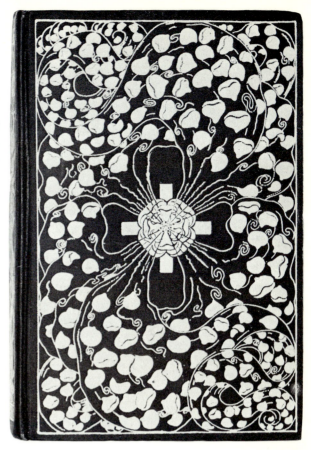

Poems
W. B. Yeats
T. Fisher Unwin, 1898
212 × 140 mm

Blocked in gold on front, spine and back on blue cloth. Binding design by Althea Giles, illustrated in *The Studio*, Winter Number 1899–1900.

Hildred: the daughter (detail)
Mrs Newton Crosland
Routledge, 1855
Depth of design 98 mm

Blocking in gold on red morocco-grain cloth, signed JL.
Collection Fianach Lawry

River Gardens (detail)
H. Noel Humphreys
Sampson Low, 1857
Depth of design 72 mm

Blocking in gold on red diagonal
wave-grain cloth.
Collection Fianach Lawry

The Adventures of Reuben Davidger
(detail)
James Greenwood
S. O. Beeton, 1865
Depth of design 115 mm

Blocking in gold on blue sand-grain
cloth, signed RD.
Collection Fianach Lawry

execution, that the nineteenth century will be able, like the fifteenth, to boast a style of its own.' Those words, it should be remembered, were spoken more than three years before the opening of the Great Exhibition, and Cundall's hopes were not fulfilled. Cundall published a further book *On Bookbindings Ancient and Modern* in 1881, but added nothing to what he had already said on publishers' bindings. Printed books, and therefore presumably publishers' bindings, were hardly shown at all in the 1851 Exhibition, owing to a mistaken official instruction that printed books were inadmissable. They were therefore not illustrated in the catalogue. In the *Art Journal Illustrated Catalogue of the International Exhibition* of 1862, there is a reproduction by wood engraving of the binding in relievo leather of Owen Jones's *Victoria Psalter*, 1861 (see p.103), and four small reproductions of designs for publishers' bindings in cloth by Bone & Son, without lettering (i.e. the illustrations were taken from the artist's designs, not the finished books). One of these is *The Poetry of Nature*, shown here on p.93. In *Masterpieces of Industrial Art and Sculpture at the International Exhibition, 1862*, J. B. Waring's three-volume work of chromolithography, one colour plate shows four bindings, including one in vellum by John Leighton, and Owen Jones's relievo leather *Holy Bible*, 1862 (see p.99), but the supporting text is woefully inadequate and uninformative.

John Hannett's *Bibliopegia* (6th edn., 1865) is a manual for hand binders and, while full of interesting information, has very little to say about edition binding in cloth, and does not mention any designers, or comment on design.

The Bookbinder, which ran as a monthly from 1888 to 1894, unfortunately changing its name to *The British Bookmaker* in 1890, has a few useful articles and a number of colour plates of cloth binding designs, but the designs chosen for illustration are mostly feeble.

After that, I have been able to find no contemporary description or appreciation of publishers' bindings at all until the 1890s. An article on *Some Recent Cloth Bookbindings* occurs in *Bookselling*, a trade publication for Christmas 1895 which is bound in off-white buckram with an elegant 'Morrisy' design in green and gold by Gleeson White, who also wrote the article. It deals only with new bindings at Christmas 1895 and is excellently illustrated: the author makes a comment on the earlier period that is condescending but perceptive: 'It is true that the covers of the past include fine designs here and there. The bindings of Luke Limner (John Leighton) are excellent of their school; others by Mr Walter Crane and Mr Lewis F. Day must not be forgotten, any more than the covers by Dante Gabriel Rossetti, which are doubtless – due credit to all others notwithstanding – the pioneers of the whole movement towards art in publishers' bindings.'

Then in 1896 *Bookbindings Old and New* was published by George Bell, in the Ex-Libris series edited by Gleeson White. The author, Brander Matthews, an American collector, devotes four chapters to Commercial Bookbinding and says that the tradition of fine leather binding was so strong in France that 'There was pressure on the designer to devise a decoration which should make his machine-made cloth cover look like the slowly tooled leather of a book bound by hand. In England, where the solid cloth-casing was hailed as a manifest improvement on the flimsy paper-boards which had immediately preceded it, there existed no such pressure ... so the designers were at liberty to develop a new form of decoration suitable to the new conditions' and adds 'there is hardly any form of modern decorative art which has achieved its aim more satisfactorily'. He also thinks that American publishers gave more thought to book-decoration than the British. He does not mention any of the mid-century designers by name, and his excellent illustrations are all of his own period.

Finally, mention must be made of *Modern Book-Bindings and Their Designers*, the winter number of *The Studio* for 1899–1900, an important and well illustrated account of what was being done in both handmade and machine-made bindings at that time in Europe (omitting Germany) and America; but it does not describe the past.

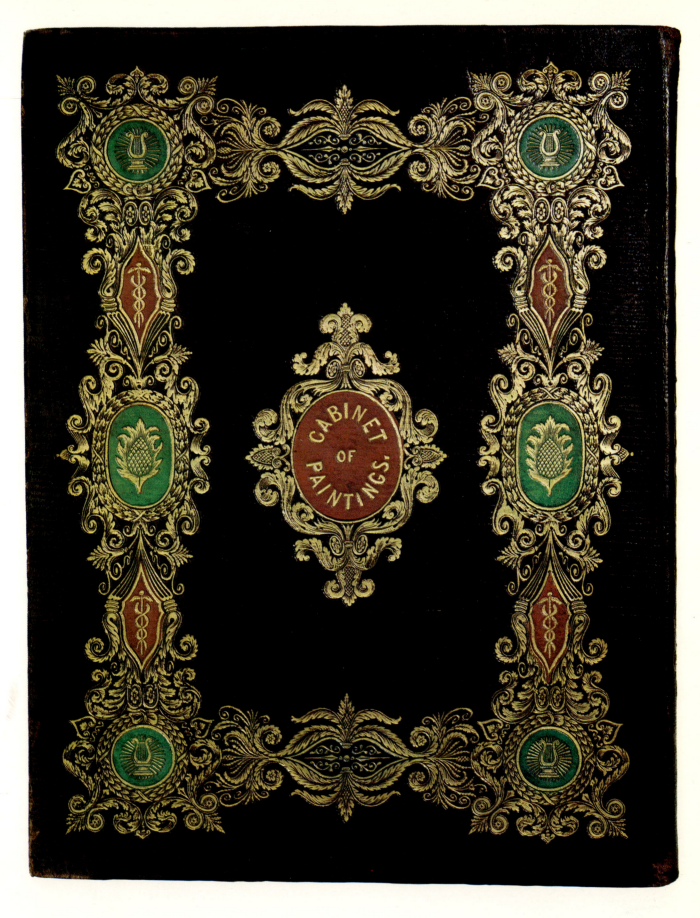

The Pictorial Album, or Cabinet of
Paintings
George Baxter
Chapman & Hall, 1837
253 × 185 mm

Dark red leather with six green, five
red, and two blue leather onlays,
blocked in gold, identical design on
front and back, blocked in gold only,
without lettering, on spine.
Collection R. de Beaumont

17

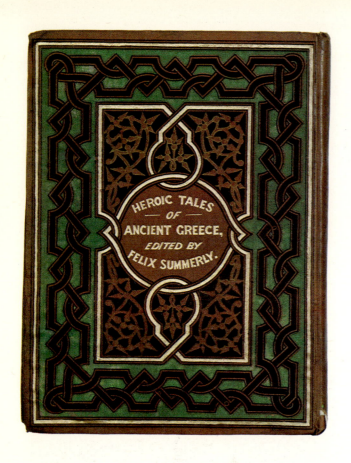

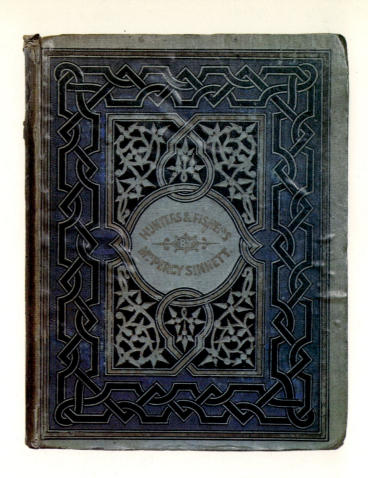

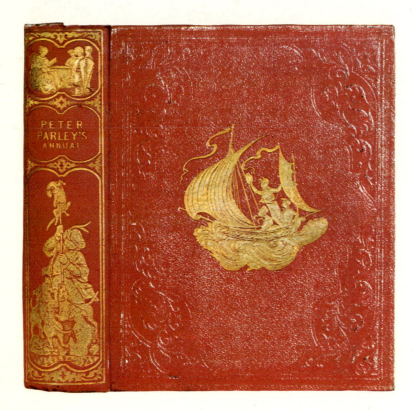

Heroic Tales of Ancient Greece
Ed. Felix Summerly
Joseph Cundall, 1844
174 × 125 mm

Brown cloth blocked in gold, green, and black on sides and spine, identical design front and back.
Collection Fianach Lawry

Hunters and Fishers
Mrs Percy Sinnett
Chapman & Hall, n.d. (*c*.1848)
178 × 128 mm

Pale blue cloth printed (from wood?) in gold, blue, and black, identical design front and back, and on spine.
 This design, similar to sixteenth-century binding designs illustrated in Shaw's *Encylopaedia of Ornament*, 1842, was probably commissioned by Joseph Cundall from the colour printers Gregory, Collins & Reynolds, whose signature appears on similar covers. It was used later by Chapman & Hall (who took over the Home Treasury copyrights from Cundall) for a series of children's books, in various colour combinations.

Peter Parley's Annual
Darton, 1848
158 × 124 mm

Crimson cloth blocked in gold and blind on front, in gold on spine, and in blind on back.

The Poetical Rhapsody, 2 volumes
Francis Davison, ed. Nicholas Harris
Nicholas. Pickering, 1826
203 × 124 mm

Reddish-brown highly glazed calico,
blocked in black, printed paper label
on spine. Pickering was the first
publisher to use cloth for binding
editions of new books, sometime in
or soon after 1820. This was a furnishing fabric; the design was hand
printed from wooden blocks.

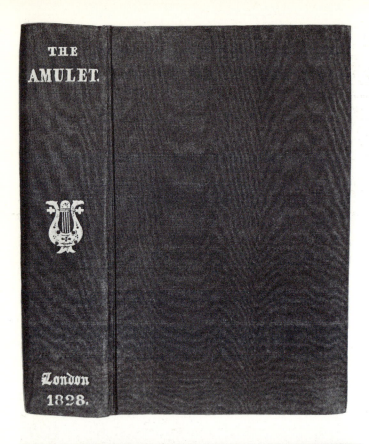

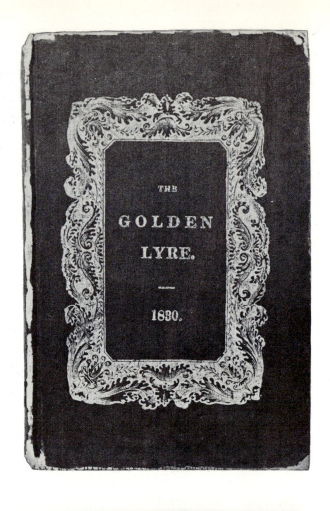

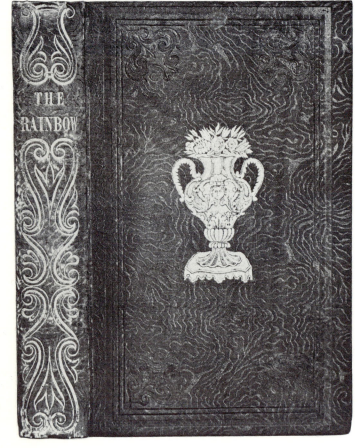

The Amulet, or Christian and Literary Remembrancer
W. Baynes & Son, and Wightman & Cramp, 1828
142 × 85 mm

Purple watered silk, blocked in gold on spine. No examples of gold blocking on cloth on books of earlier date than this are known to exist. This book was issued in an elegant paper-on-boards decorated slipcase, at 12s.

The Golden Lyre, second series
Ed. J. Macray
J. D. Haas, 1830
150 × 94 mm

Watered blue silk (probably a dress fabric) blocked in gold on front only.
  The text of this little book was printed in gold throughout, on one side only of coated paper, by Howlett & Brimmer, 10 Frith Street, Soho.
Collection R. de Beaumont

The Rainbow
Henry Glasford Bell
London, Smith & Company (Smith, Elder & Co., Cornhill), n.d. (*c.*1830)
190 × 117 mm

Patterned crimson silk blocked in blind and gold, signed on blind panel J. J. Smith, Binder, Gate Street, (identical design on front and back) and in gold on spine.
  The author states on page 69 that he was writing 'between the hours of twelve and one of Friday the 14th August, eighteen hundred and thirty'.
Collection C. Dobson

Forget Me Not
Ed. Frederic Shoberl
R. Ackermann, 1830
148 × 90 mm

Crimson watered silk blocked in gold, identical design front and back, and on spine. This annual was issued in a beautiful coloured gold-blocked paper-on-board slipcase.

The Book of Common Prayer
Cambridge, 1830
143 × 78 mm

Black leather blocked in blind,
identical design front and back, and
in gold and blind on spine. Signed
REMNANT & EDMONDS
Collection R. de Beaumont

Album
Remnant & Edmonds, 1830
245 × 190 mm

Green leather blocked in blind,
identical design front and back, and
in gold and blind on spine. Signed
REMNANT & EDMONDS LON-
DON.

21

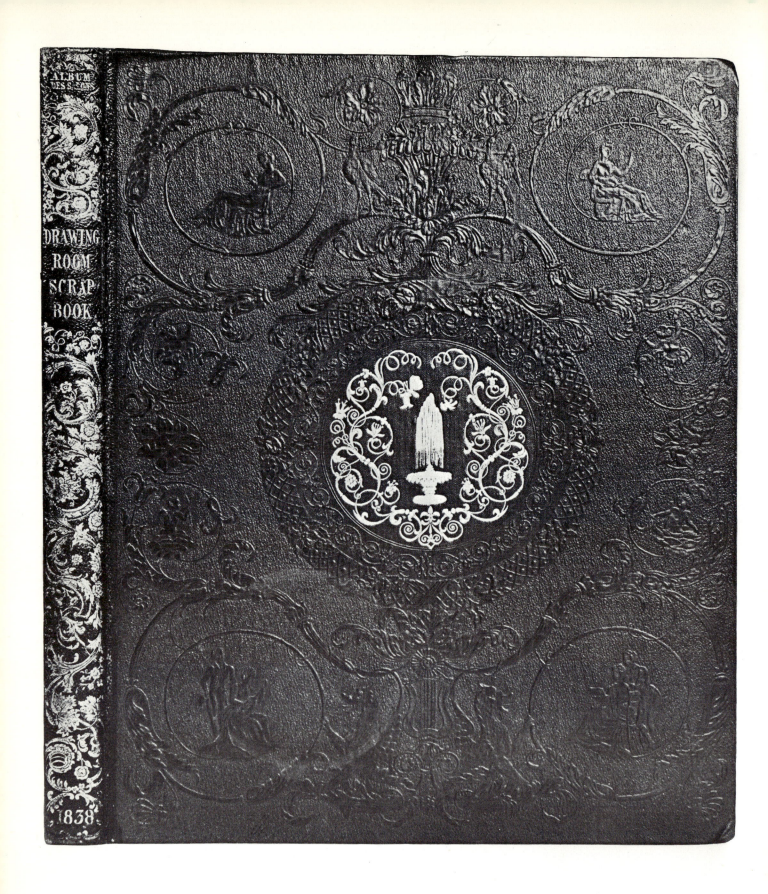

Fisher's Drawing Room Scrap Book,
1838
Fisher, Son & Co., 1838
285 × 220 mm

Green leather spine blocked in gold, green cloth sides blocked in blind and gold, identical design on front and back. (The same spine in gold, and blind block on the sides, was used on the 1837 *Scrap Book*, on different coloured cloth and with a different roundel in gold on the sides.)
Collection C. Dobson

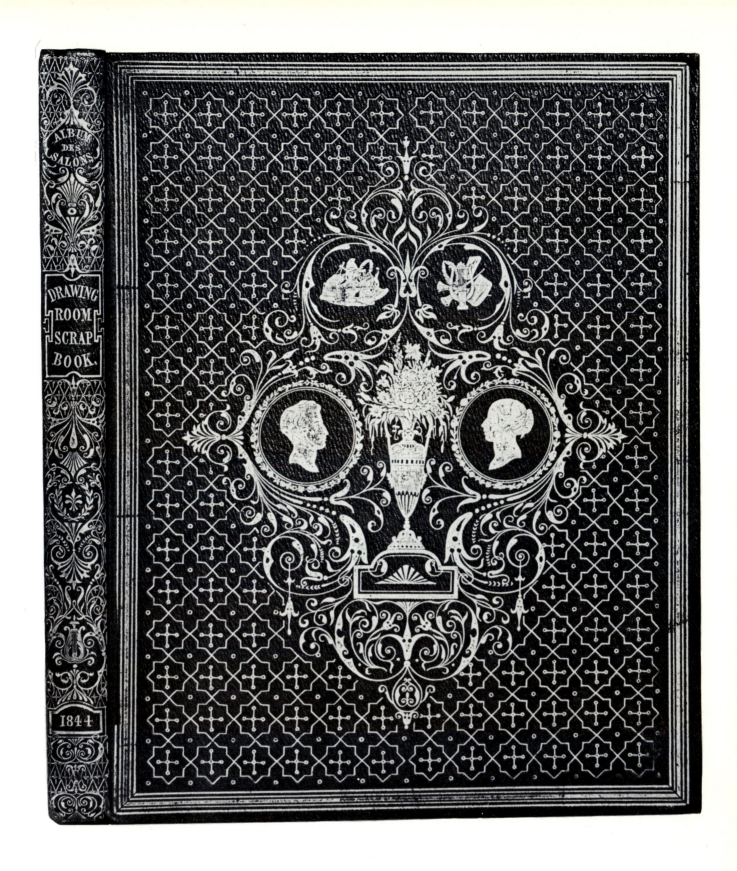

Fisher's Drawing Room Scrap Book,
1844
Fisher, Son & Co.
280 × 215 mm

Blue cloth blocked in gold on sides
and spine, identical design on front
and back; spine design same as on
1851.
Collection C. Dobson

Fisher's Drawing Room Scrap Book,
1851
Fisher, Son & Co., 1851
295 × 228 mm

Magenta morocco-grained cloth
blocked in gold, identical design
front and back, and on spine (which
was repeated from 1844).

24

The Tourist in Spain
Thomas Roscoe, ill. David Roberts
R. Jennings, 1837
245 × 154 mm

Red morocco blocked in gold.

The Clan Maclean
A. Seneachie
Smith, Elder & Co., 1838
230 × 140 mm

Dark green or blue cloth blocked in blind on front, back, and spine, and in gold on spine. The floral design and ribbed background blocked on to the cloth extends over the edges of the book, showing that the cloth was not made specially for this book.

26

Ireland Picturesque and Romantic
Leith Ritchie, ill. D. McClise and
T. Creswick
Longman, 1838
244 × 165 mm

Green cotton plush blocked in blind
on sides and spine (probably from a
heated copper plate) identical design
front and back, with blue cloth
labels on spine blocked in gold. The
design is not a continuous one, like
that on the facing page, but was
clearly made for a book cover of this
size.

The Passion of Our Lord Jesus Christ portrayed by Albert Dürer
Ed. Henry Cole
Joseph Cundall, 1844
203 × 135 mm

Red morocco, blocked in blind with gilt metal clasp, corner, and centre-pieces, identical design front and back, probably by Hayday. Copies were also issued with the same design blocked in blind on both brown leather and cloth, minus the metal embellishments. (This copy re-backed.)
Collection R. de Beaumont

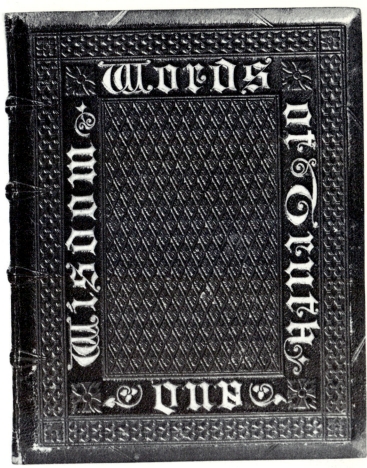

The Sermon on the Mount
Illuminated by Owen Jones
Longman, 1845
172 × 120 mm

Pure red silk, draw-loom woven to
shape of book, lettering on spine in-
corporated in woven design, bevelled
boards. The design follows the general
style of early seventeenth-century
book covers. The silk covers were
probably woven in Spitalfields. This
binding was also made in a gold and
white colour scheme.
Collection Fianach Lawry

Words of Truth and Wisdom
Joseph Cundall (*c.* 1848)
168 × 127 mm

Brown leather tooled (or blocked?) in
gold and blind by Hayday.

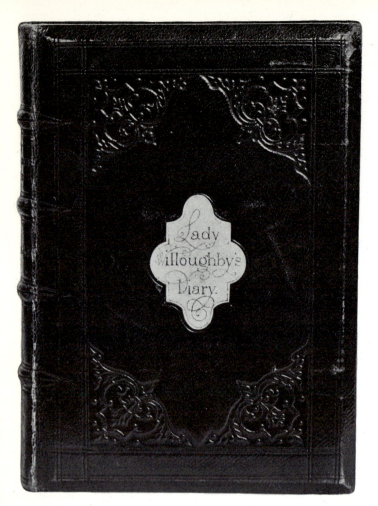

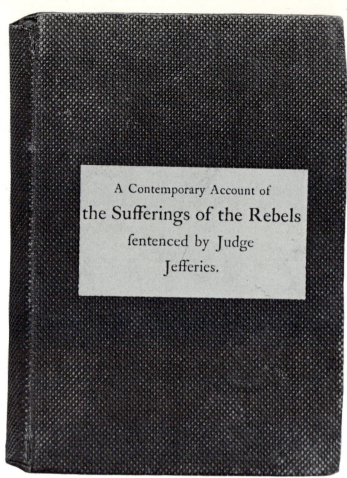

Lady Willoughby's Diary, 4th edition
Longman, 1846
170 × 112 mm

Dark red morocco tooled or blocked
in blind, with cut out vellum or paper
panel onlay hand-lettered in red and
black on front and back. Gold basket-
work gauffering on all edges. Signed
Hayday.

The Sufferings of the Rebels (on title-
page: *A Memorandum of the
Wonderful Providence of God, etc.*)
John Coad
Longman, 1849
160 × 110 mm

Black fine bead-grained cloth with
white paper label printed in black,
pasted on front, nothing on spine or
back.
Collection Fianach Lawry

The Preacher
Illum. Owen Jones
Longman, 1849
292 × 193 mm

Wood sides (with leather spine) heat-stamped (not carved) by Remnant & Edmonds after design by Owen Jones. This is the only book cover known to have been produced by this process. The book was also published with the same design stamped on crimson leather and cloth.

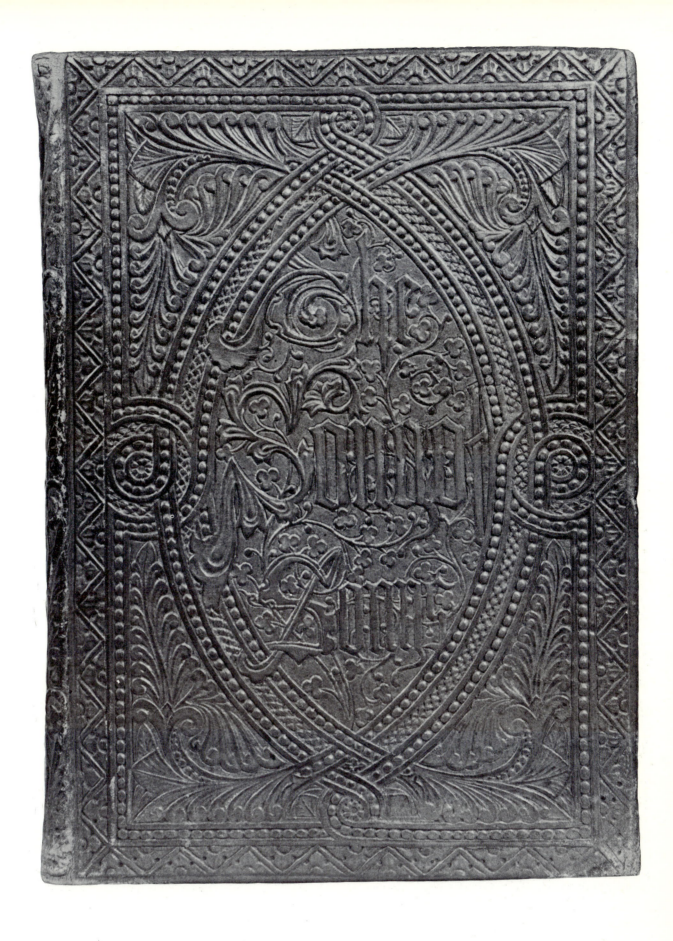

Flowers and their kindred thoughts
Illum. Owen Jones
Longman, 1848
267 × 180 mm

Brown *relievo* leather, designs by
Owen Jones, different on front and
back. On these covers the design is
sunk into the surface of the leather.

The Song of Songs
Illum. Owen Jones
Longman, 1849
210 × 146 mm

Brown *relievo* leather, designs by
Owen Jones, different on front and
back, and on spine. The design is in
relief, higher than the surface of the
leather.

The Book of British Ballads, 2nd series
Ed. S. C. Hall
Jeremiah How, 1844
270 × 186 mm

White cloth printed (from wood?) in
blue and gold on front, back, and
spine.
Collection R. de Beaumont

34

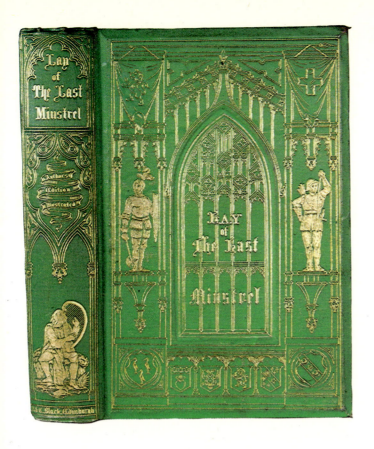

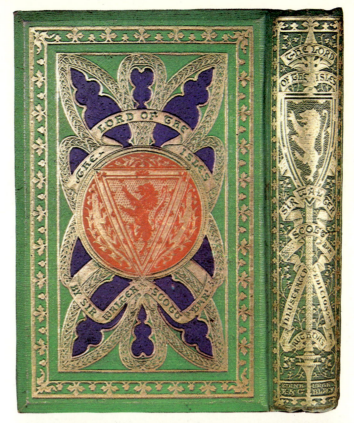

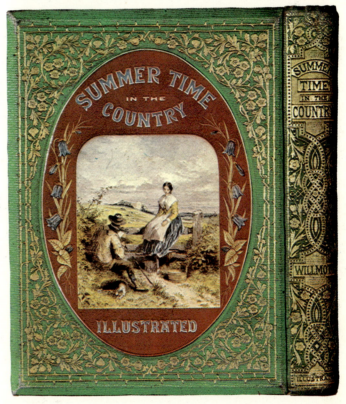

The Lay of the Last Minstrel
Sir W. Scott, ill. B. Foster and
  J. Gilbert
A. & C. Black, 1854
219 × 133 mm

Emerald green leather-grained cloth
blocked in gold with sunk panel,
identical design front and back,
bevelled boards, in gold on spine.
This book also appeared in crimson
cloth.

The Lord of the Isles
Sir W. Scott, ill. B. Foster and
  J. Gilbert
A. & C. Black, 1857
219 × 133 mm

Red cloth with blue and green paper
onlays, blocked in gold, identical
design front and back, in gold on
spine. Label: Leighton Son & Hodge.
  Two splendid examples of Victorian
Gothic, unsigned but almost certainly
by John Leighton.

Summer Time in the Country
R. A. Willmott, ill. B. Foster *et al.*
Routledge, 1858
205 × 146 mm

Emerald green cloth blocked in gold,
with oval paper onlay printed in
colours from wood by Edmund
Evans, after a drawing by B. Foster,
identical design front and back, gold
only on spine, bevelled boards.

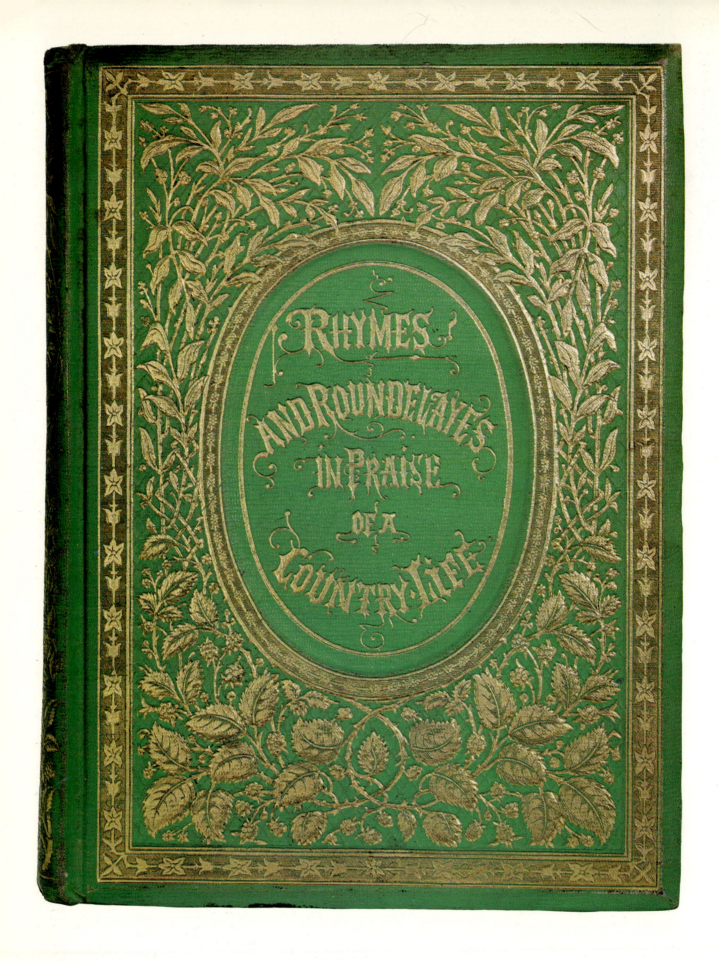

Rhymes and Roundelayes in praise of a country life
Ed. Joseph Cundall
Bogue, 1857
234 × 160 mm

Emerald green cloth blocked in gold and blind, with oval sunk panel, identical design front and back, in gold only on spine, bevelled boards. The background to the floral design round the oval is blocked with trellis-work in blind, a refinement which is hardly visible in the reproduction. The rustic lettering is vigorous.
Collection C. Dobson

The Artist's Married Life, being that of Albert Dürer
Translated from the German of L. Schefer by Mrs J. R. Stodart
John Chapman, 1848
172 × 108 mm

Yellow or brown cloth printed (from wood?) in gold and black. Signed Collins & Reynolds, on heavily bevelled boards.
Collection R. de Beaumont

Insect Changes
H. Noel Humphreys
Grant & Griffith, 1847
175 × 121 mm

Fawn cloth printed (from wood?) in gold, black, and brown, after a design by Holbein.

A Popular Account of Discoveries at Nineveh
Austen Henry Layard
John Murray, 1851
197 × 127 mm

Pink cloth printed from type and wood in black, on front, back, and spine.
Collection R. de Beaumont

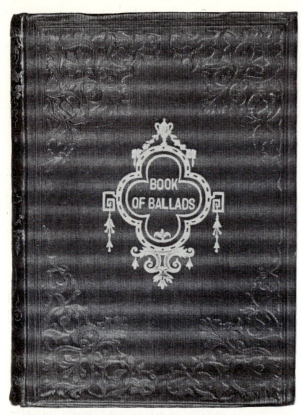

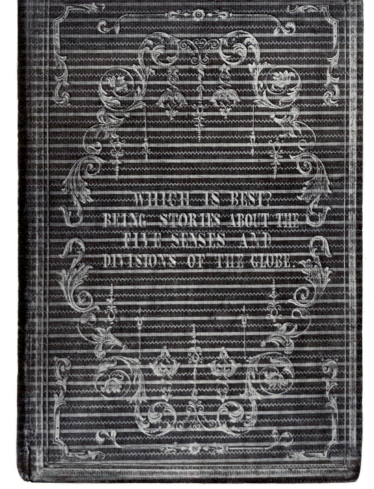

The Book of Ballads
Ed. Bon Gautier, ill. Alfred Crow-
quill
W. S. Orr, 1845
158 × 106 mm

Blue fine-ribbed cloth with dark blue
horizontal stripes, blocked in gold
and blind on front and spine, in
blind on back.
Collection R. de Beaumont

The Book of Ballads
Ed. Bon Gautier, ill. Alfred Crow-
quill
W. S. Orr, 1845
158 × 106 mm

The same book as above, but in red
fine-ribbed cloth with dark red
vertical stripes.
Collection C. Dobson

The Sicilian Vespers
Rev. C. Smyth
E. Palmer & Son, 1848
175 × 105 mm

Purple diagonal-ribbed cloth with
lighter horizontal stripes, blocked in
gold on spine, in blind on front and
back.
Collection Fianach Lawry

Which is Best?
Thomas Dean, n.d. (c. 1848)
180 × 117 mm

Yellow ribbed cloth printed with
horizontal stripes in green, blocked
in gold. The same pattern of stripes
is printed on similar cloth on a book
published by Nelson in 1848.
Collection Fianach Lawry

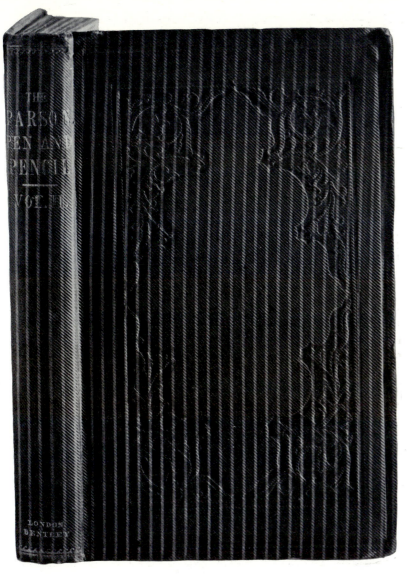

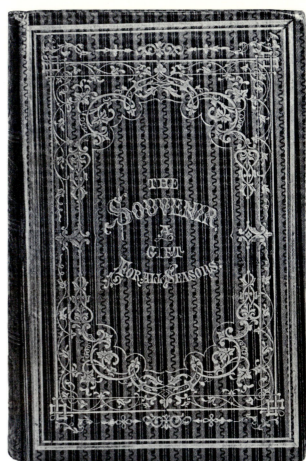

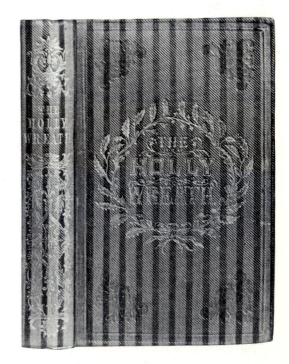

The Parson, Pen & Pencil
G. M. Musgrave
Bentley, 3 volumes, 1848
206 × 117 mm

Maroon diagonal-ribbed cloth, with vertical dark blue stripes, blocked in blind on front, gold on spine.

Examples of similar striped calicoes were shown in *The Journal of Design*, March 1849, manufactured by Cussons & Co., 51 Bunhill Row, for W. Bone & Son, 76 Fleet Street.

The Souvenir
T. Nelson, 1849
165 × 100 mm

Olive green wavy pattern cloth with vertical stripes printed in dark brown (?) and blocked in gold on front and spine, in blind on back.
Collection R. de Beaumont

The Holly Wreath: a fireside companion for a winter's evening
Anne Maria Sargeant
H. G. Collins, n.d. (inscribed 1851)
165 × 100 mm

Red diagonal-ribbed cloth with black vertical stripes, blocked in gold and blind on front and spine, blind on back.
Collection R. de Beaumont

Lalla Rookh
T. Moore
Longman, 1851
222 × 152 mm

Blue fine ripple cloth with light blue
stripes, blocked in gold and blind on
spine, in blind on front and back.
Bound by Westleys & Co., Friar
Street, London.
Collection Fianach Lawry

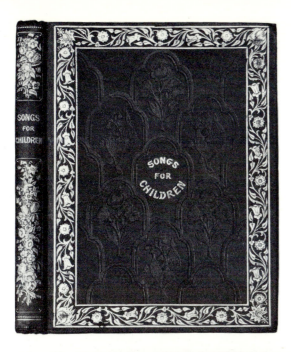

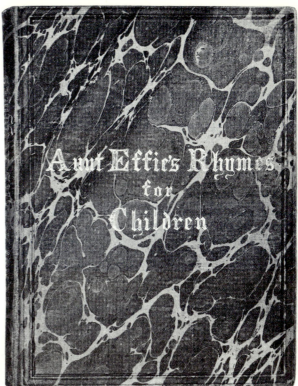

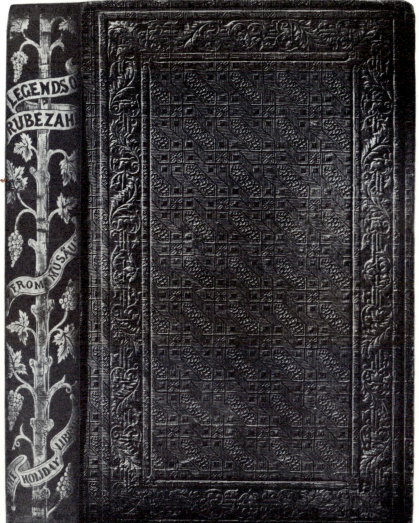

Aunt Effie's Rhymes for Little Children
Ill. H. K. Browne
Addey & Co., n.d. (*c.*1852)
190 × 140 mm

Green fine ripple cloth printed with marble pattern in red, blocked in gold on front and spine.
Collection R. de Beaumont

Songs for Children
Ill. B. Foster
W. S. Orr, 1850
187 × 140 mm

Dark green ribbed cloth blocked in gold and blind on front and spine.

Legends of Rubezahl
Cundall, 1845
178 × 108 mm

Blue cloth with two separate blockings in blind on front and back, in gold on spine.

The History of Emily and her Mother
Mrs Sherwood
Houlston & Stoneman, 1852
148 × 92 mm

Green cloth with two separate blockings in blind on front and back, in gold on spine.
Collection R. de Beaumont

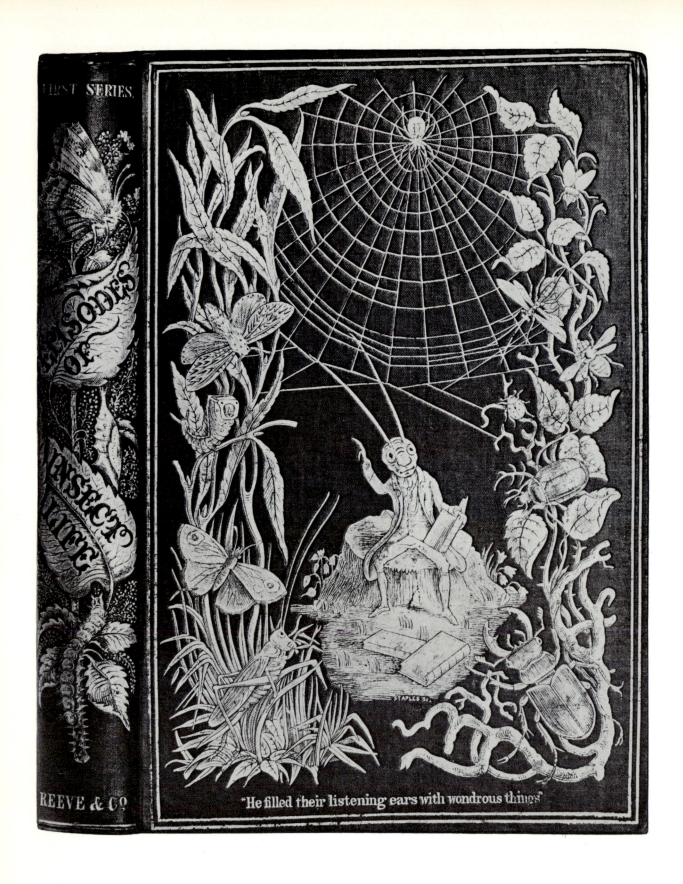

"He filled their listening ears with wondrous things"

Episodes of Insect Life, 2nd series
Acheta Domestica, M.E.S. (Miss E. L.
  Budgen)
Reeve, Benham & Reeve, King
  William Street, Strand, 1849
208 × 136 mm

Blue ribbed cloth blocked in gold on
front, back, and spine. Signed
STAPLES SC. Label: Bound by
Westleys & Co., Friar Street,
London
Collection R. de Beaumont

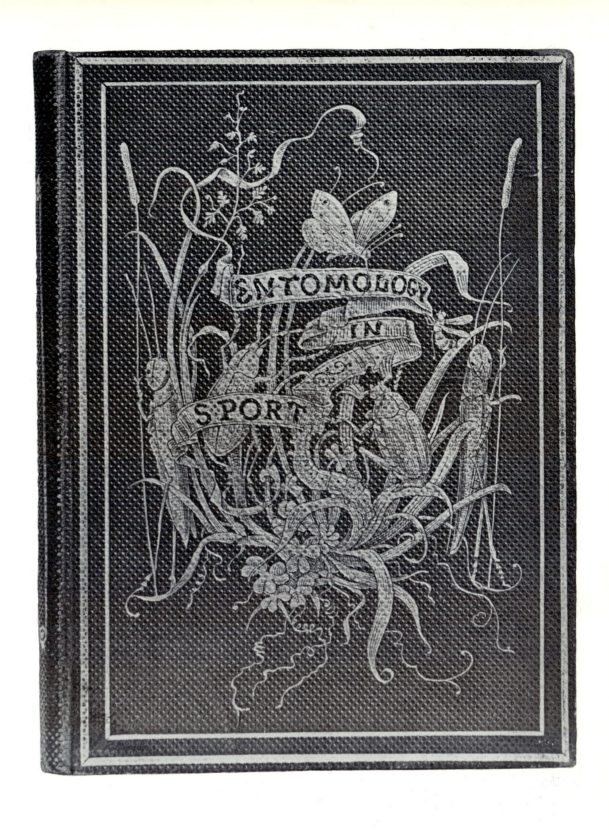

Entomology in Sport
Paul Jerrard, n.d. (*c.*1859)
190 × 137 mm

Blue bead grain cloth blocked in gold
on front and spine, in blind on back.
Collection Fianach Lawry

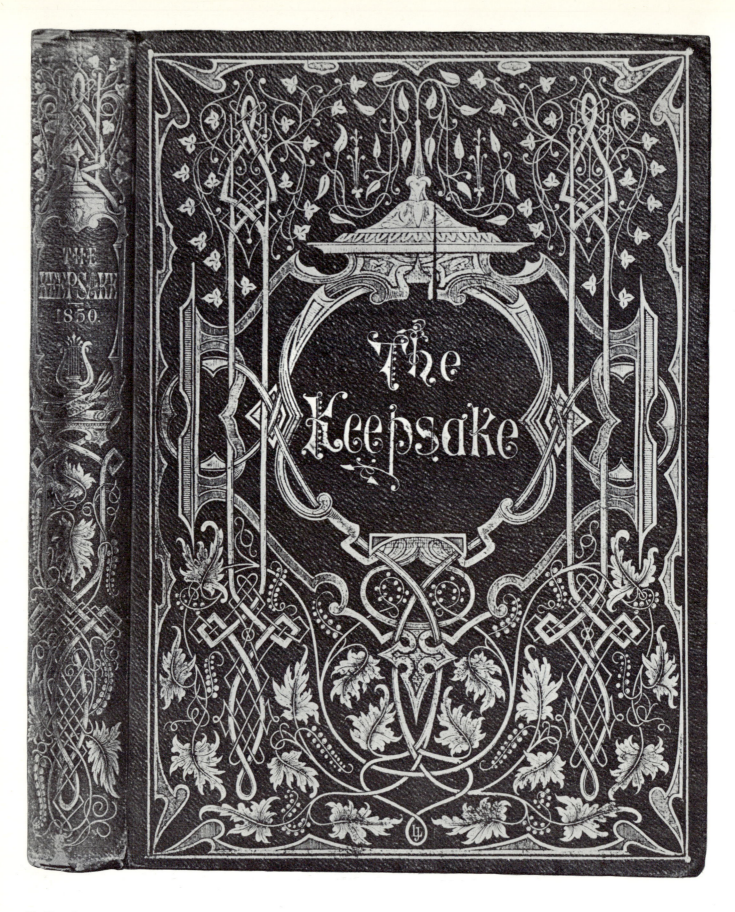

The Keepsake 1850
Ed. the late Countess of Blessington
David Bogue, 1850
245 × 170 mm

Red cloth blocked in gold on front
and spine, in blind on back, signed
JL – the initials of John Leighton
(1822–1912), the most prolific designer
of book covers of the nineteenth
century. The earliest designs signed
by him are of 1845.
Collection R. de Beaumont

The Court Album
David Bogue, 1853
298 × 220 mm

Emerald green sand-grain cloth
blocked in gold (identical on front
and back) on both sides and spine.
Signed JL.
Collection C. Dobson

'Excelsior'
Alastor (James Orton)
William Pickering, 1852
198 × 140 mm

Blue wavy grain cloth blocked in
gold on front, spine, and back
(identical on front and back).
Signed WHR (W. Harry Rogers).
Label: Bone & Son, Binder.
  A very peculiar design, one of the
earliest signed by Rogers.
Collection John Porter

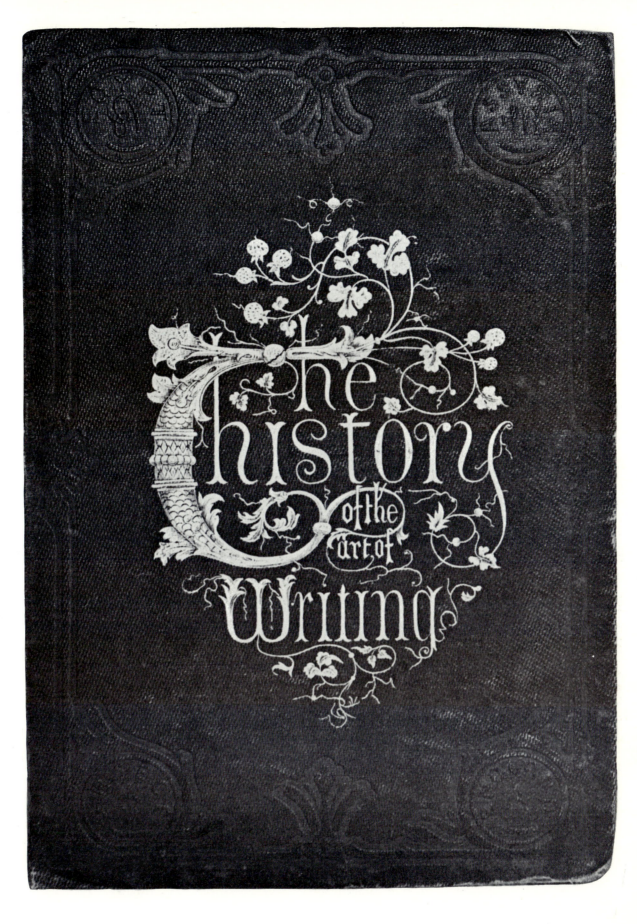

*The Origin and Progress of the Art of
Writing*
H. N. Humphreys
Ingram, Cooke, 1853
265 × 175 mm

Blue ripple-grained cloth blocked in
gold and blind on front and spine, in
blind on back. Presumably designed
by H.N.H. but unsigned.
Collection Fianach Lawry

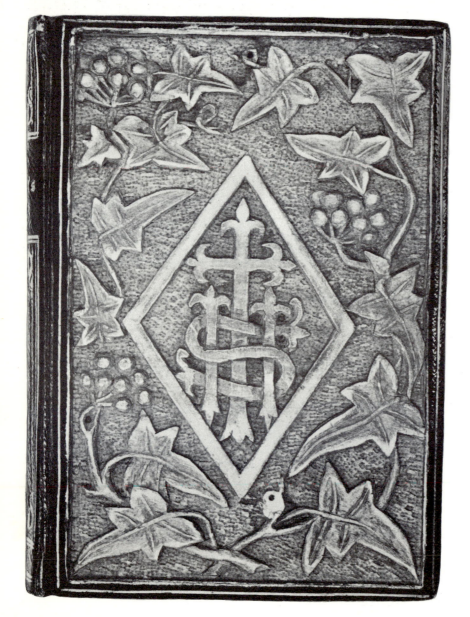

Irish Scenery: Belfast
Ormiston & Glass, 8 Elder Street,
Edinburgh, n.d.
102 × 142 mm

Mauchline ware: varnished wood
with pictorial transfer in black.
Collection Fianach Lawry

*The Mothers legacie to her Unborne
childe*
Elizabeth Ioceline.
Reprinted from the edition of 1625
W. Blackwood, Edinburgh, 1853
141 × 98 mm

Carved wood panels, front and back
different, inlaid on blue leather, tooled
in gold on spine and on bevelled
edges. May or may not have been an
edition binding.
Collection R. de Beaumont

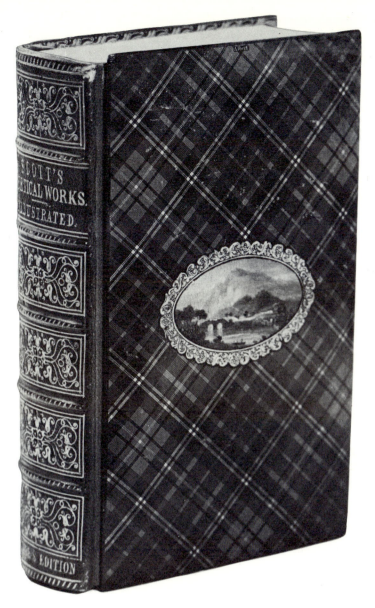

The Poetical Works of Sir Walter Scott
A. & C. Black, Edinburgh, 1853
175 × 102 mm

Mauchline ware: varnished wood sides, tartan paper onlay, with (?) hand-painted view in oval on front. Green leather spine blocked in gold. 'Albert', blocked in gold at top of front cover, is the name of tartan.
Collection Fianach Lawry

The Poetical Works of Longfellow
T. Nelson, Edinburgh, 1871
168 × 108

Mauchline ware: varnished wood sides with fern designs. Green leather spine blocked in gold.
Collection Fianach Lawry

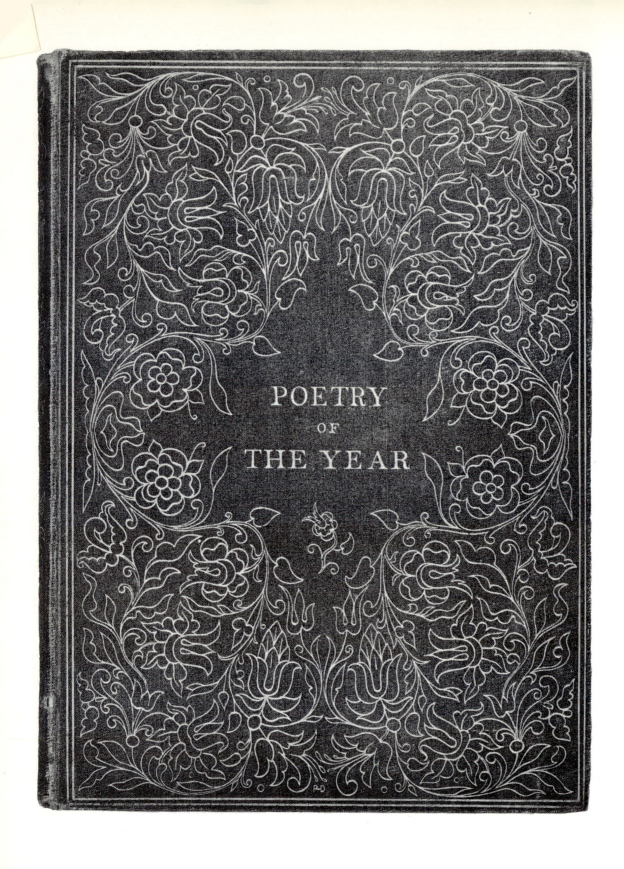

Poetry of the Year
G. Bell, 1853
285 × 200 mm

Emerald green cloth blocked in gold
on front and spine, in blind on back.
Signed (P.D. or) R.D. R. D. were the
initials of Robert Dudley.

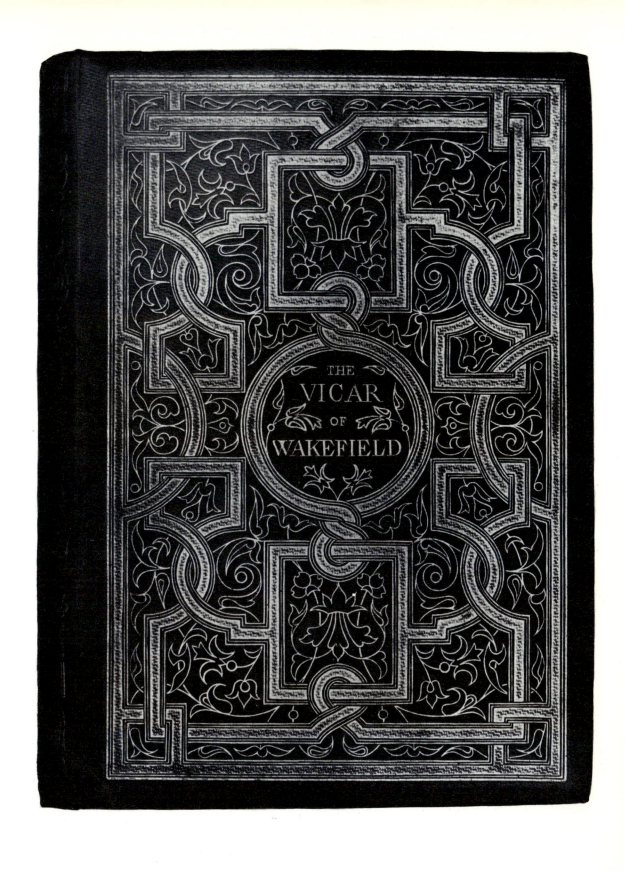

The Vicar of Wakefield
O. Goldsmith
For Joseph Cundall by Sampson Low
1855
210 × 140 mm

Orange cloth blocked in gold on
front and spine, in blind on back.
Signed W.H.R. (W. Harry Rogers).
Bound by Bone & Son.

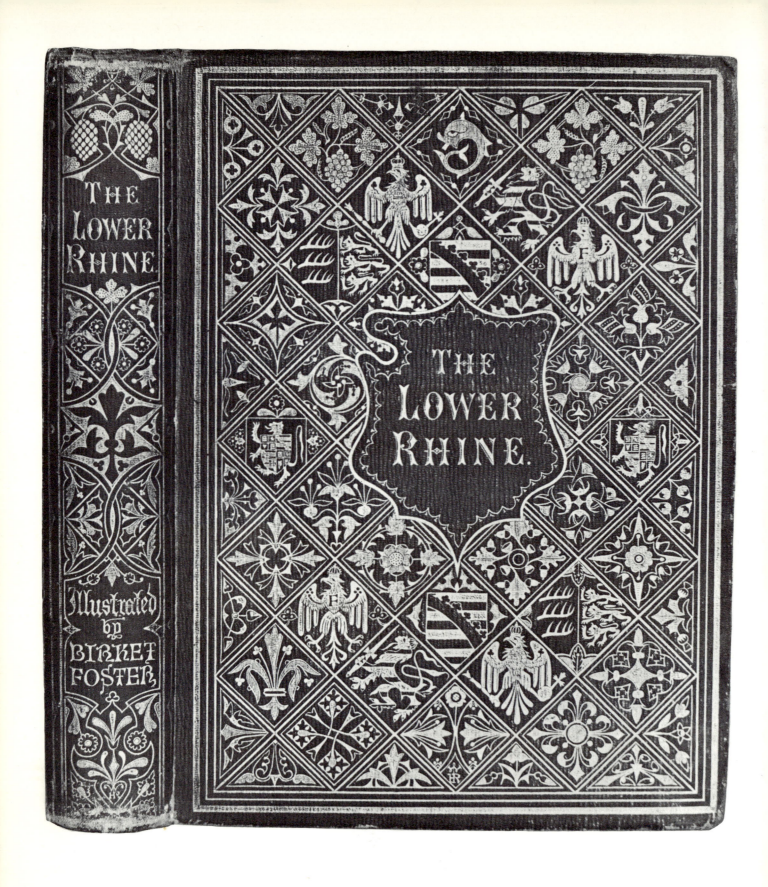

The Rhine (*Rotterdam to Maience*)
H. Mayhew, ill. by B. Foster
D. Bogue, 1856
240 × 170 mm

Blue morocco-grained cloth blocked
in gold, identical design front, back,
and on spine. Signed W.H.R.
Collection Fianach Lawry

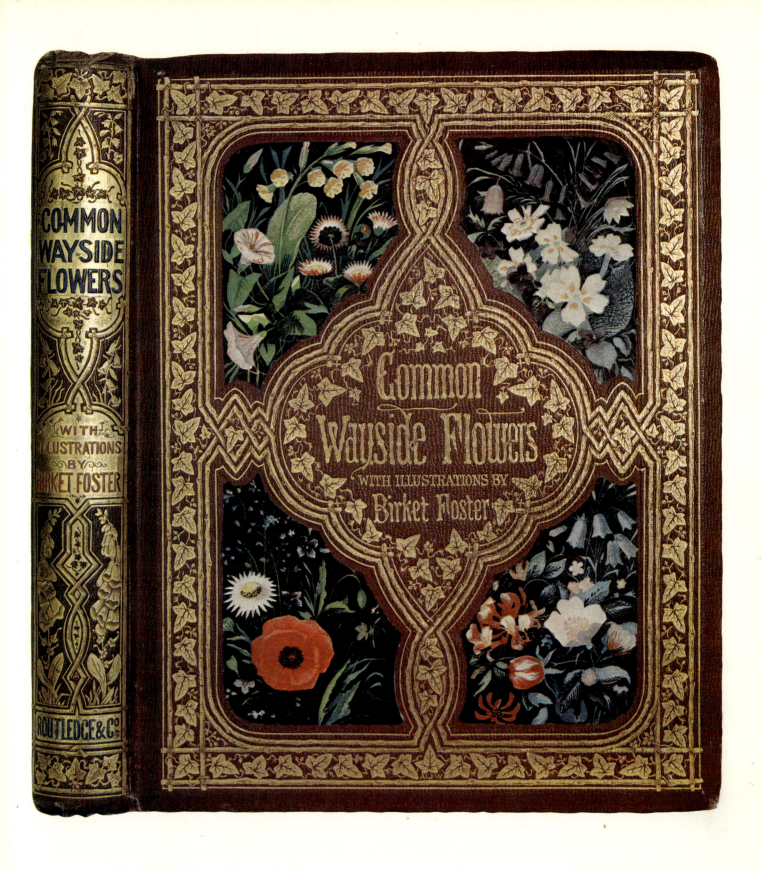

Common Wayside Flowers
T. Miller, ill. B. Foster
Routledge, Warne & Routledge,
1860
228 × 172 mm

Brown leather-grained cloth blocked
in gold with four cut-out paper
onlays printed in colours from wood
by Edmund Evans, identical design
front and back. Signed AW. Spine
with two blue and one red paper
onlays blocked in gold, bevelled
boards. Label: Bound by Bone &
Son, 76 Fleet Street, London.
 Perhaps the most sensational of all
the cut-out paper and gold blocking
bindings.

53

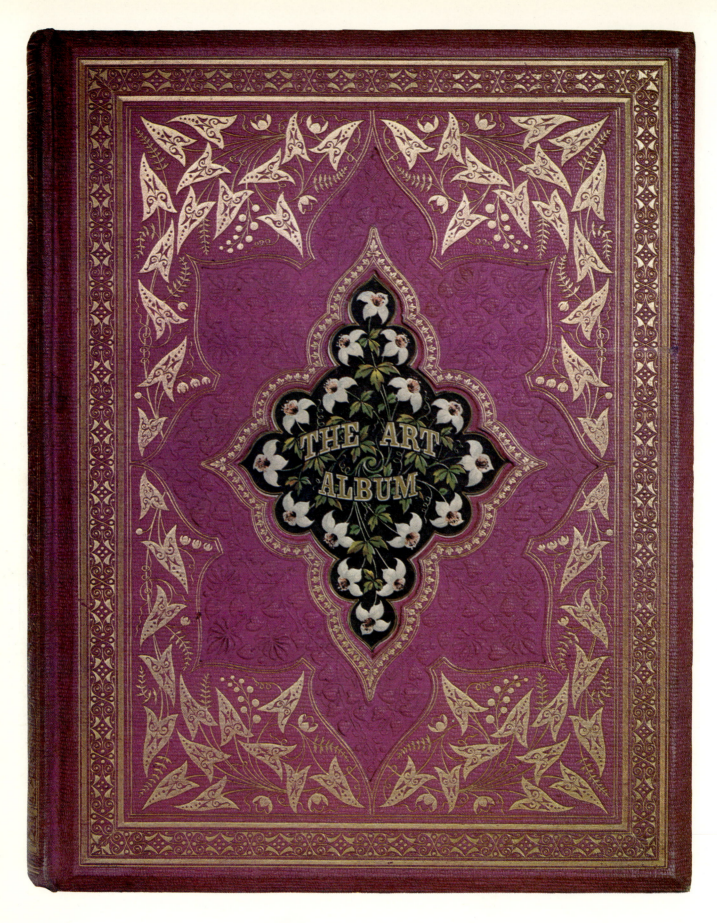

The Art Album
W. Kent, 1861
268 × 196 mm

Purple leather-grained cloth blocked
in gold and blind, with cut-out paper
onlay printed in colours, identical
design front and back, in gold only
on spine, bevelled boards.
  Unsigned, but close to the style of
Albert Warren.
Collection R. de Beaumont

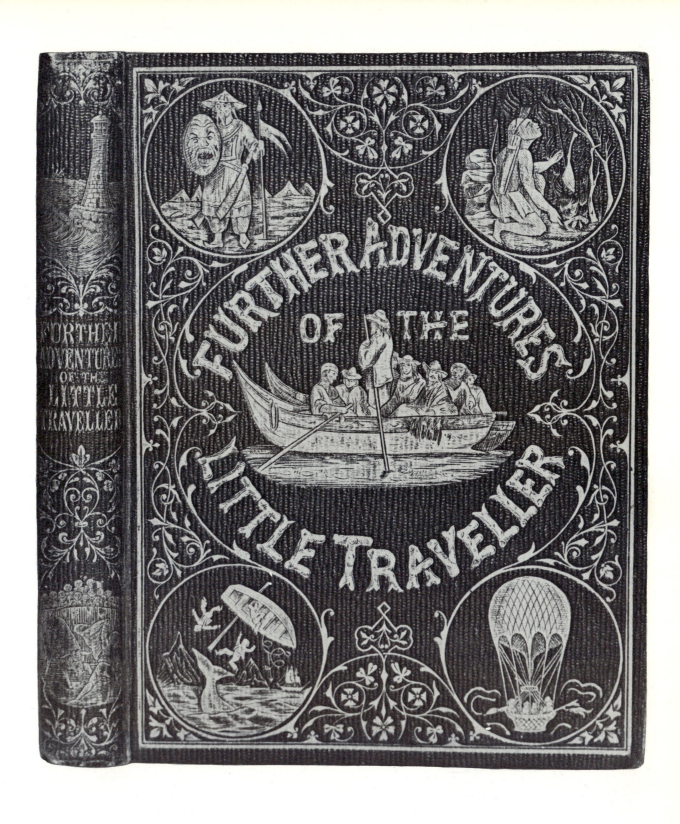

The Further Adventures of the Little Traveller
Blackwood, 1857
182 × 133 mm

Blue morocco-grained cloth blocked in gold on front and spine, in blind on back. Pictorial block in centre of cover. Signed HOARE.
Collection R. de Beaumont

Christmas with the Poets, 3rd edition
Ill. B. Foster
D. Bogue, 1855
248 × 165 mm

Red cloth with deep embossed panels,
blocked in gold, identical design front
and back, blocked in gold on spine,
bevelled boards. Label: Leighton Son
& Hodge, Shoe Lane, London.
Collection R. de Beaumont

Sakoontala etc.
Monier Williams,
Stephen Austin, Hertford, 1855
230 × 172 mm

Dark green leather blocked in gold
on front, back, and spine. Signed
T. SULMAN INVT KNIGHTS &
KEELING SC
 This book, with the same binding
design, was issued in different
coloured leathers, including white,
and with gauffered edges.

The Gulistan of Sadi
Transl. E. B. Eastwick
Stephen Austin, Hertford, 1852
222 × 140 mm

Emerald green ripple cloth blocked in
gold with same design on front and
back, and in gold on spine.
Collection Fianach Lawry

The Traveller
O. Goldsmith, ill. Birket Foster
D. Bogue, n.d. (*c.*1868)
225 × 146 mm

Red cloth blocked in gold and blind
on front, spine and back, bevelled
boards.
Collection Fianach Lawry

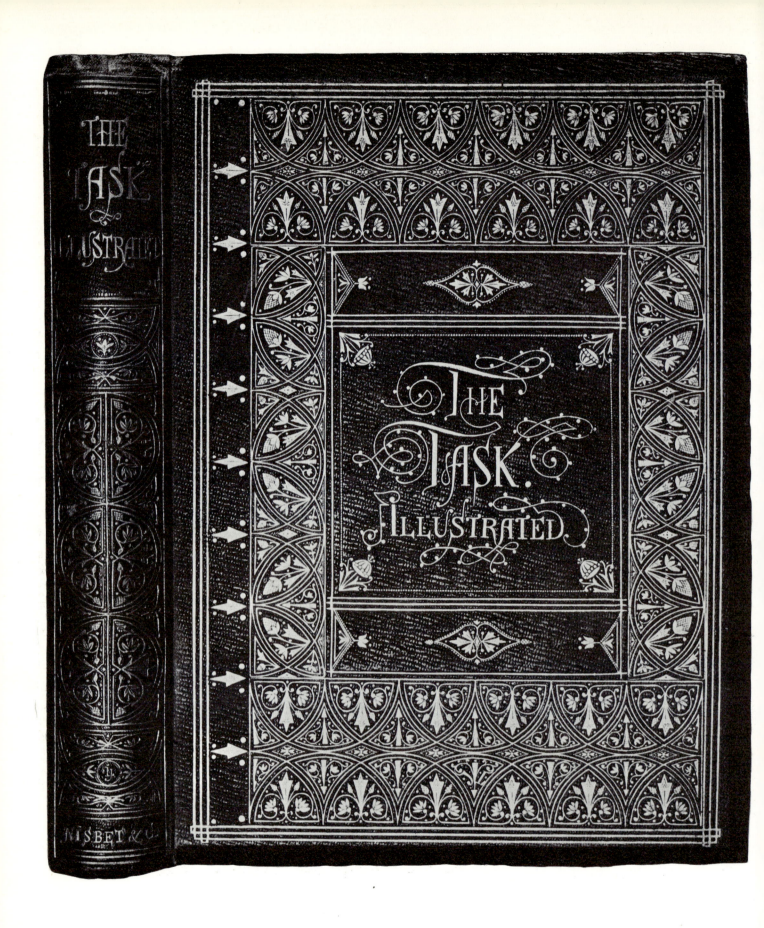

The Task
W. Cowper, ill. B. Foster
Nisbet, 1855
212 × 150 mm

Emerald green morocco-grained
cloth blocked in gold on front and
spine, bevelled boards. Signed JL.
Label: Edmonds & Remnant, London.

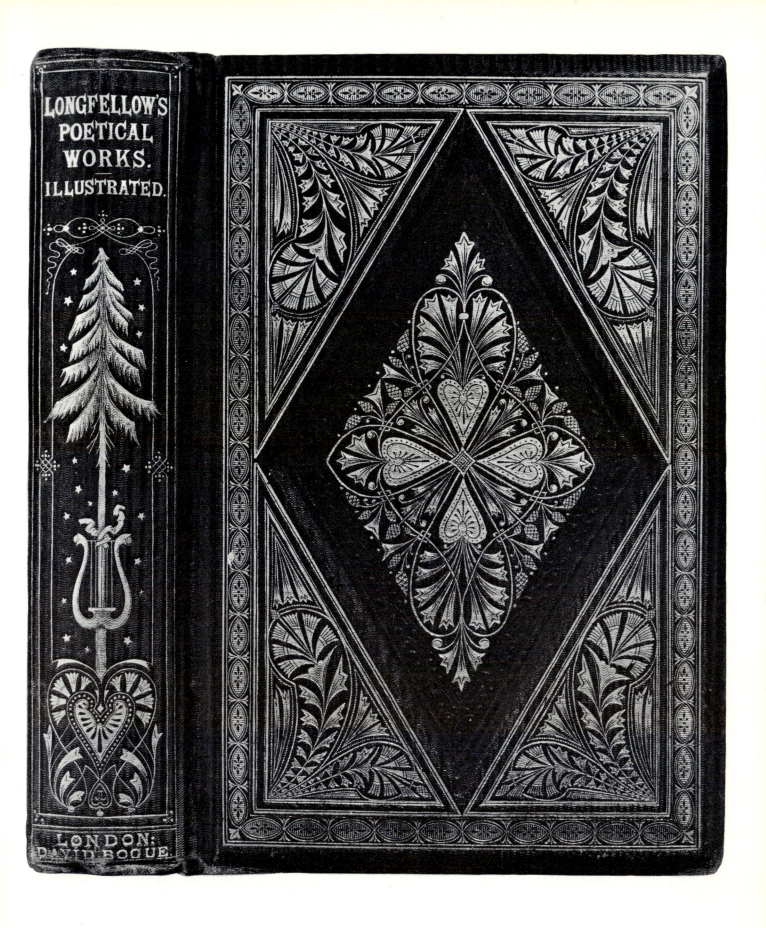

Poetical Works
H. Longfellow
D. Bogue, 1856
216 × 140 mm

Blue ripple cloth, blocked in gold and
blind on front, in gold on spine,
bevelled boards. Signed JL. Label:
Leighton Son & Hodge, Shoe Lane,
London.
Collection Fianach Lawry

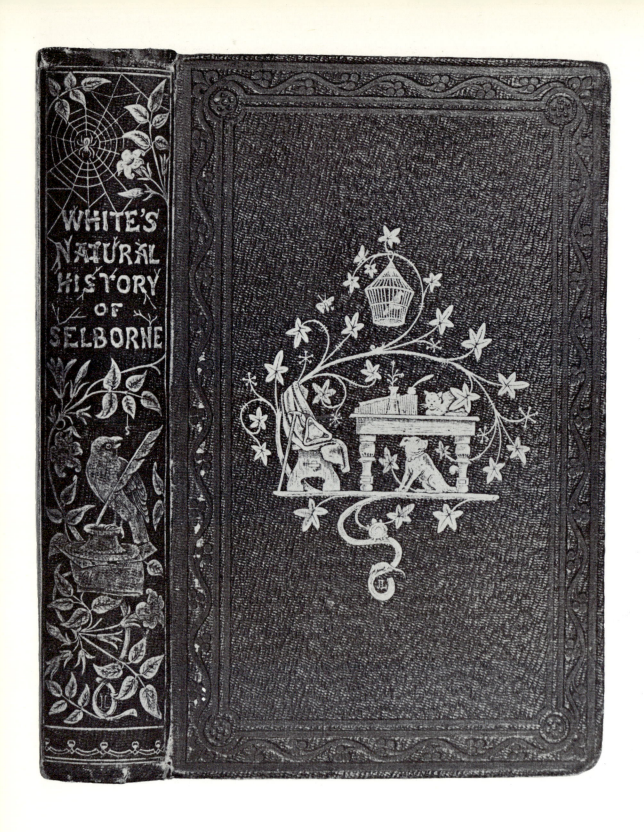

The Natural History of Selborne
G. White
Routledge, 1854
190 × 118 mm

Blue leather-grained cloth blocked
in gold and blind on front, in gold on
spine. Signed JL.
Collection Fianach Lawry

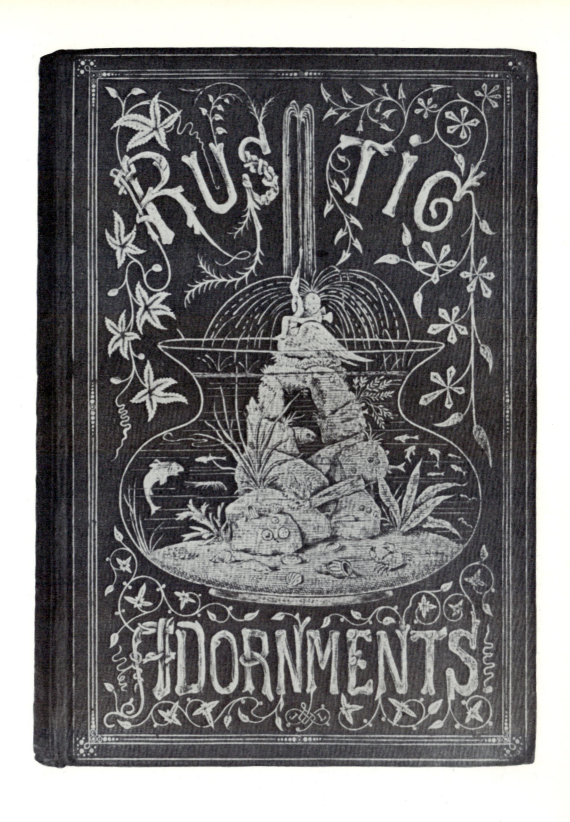

Rustic Adornments for Homes of Taste
Shirley Hibberd
Groombridge, 1856
190 × 124 mm

Emerald green cloth blocked in gold,
identical design on front back, and
on spine. Signed JL. Bound by
Westleys.

March Winds and April Showers
'Acheta'
Lovell Reeve, 1854
With *May Flowers*, by 'Acheta', 1855.
175 × 115 mm

Red fine-grained cloth blocked in
gold and blind on front and spine.
Collection Fianach Lawry

64

Angelo; or, the Pine Forest in the Alps
(enlarged detail)
Geraldine E. Jewsbury, ill. John
 Absolon
Grant & Griffith, 1856.

Red grained cloth blocked in gold
and blind. Signed JL.
Depth of design 98 mm.
Collection Fianach Lawry

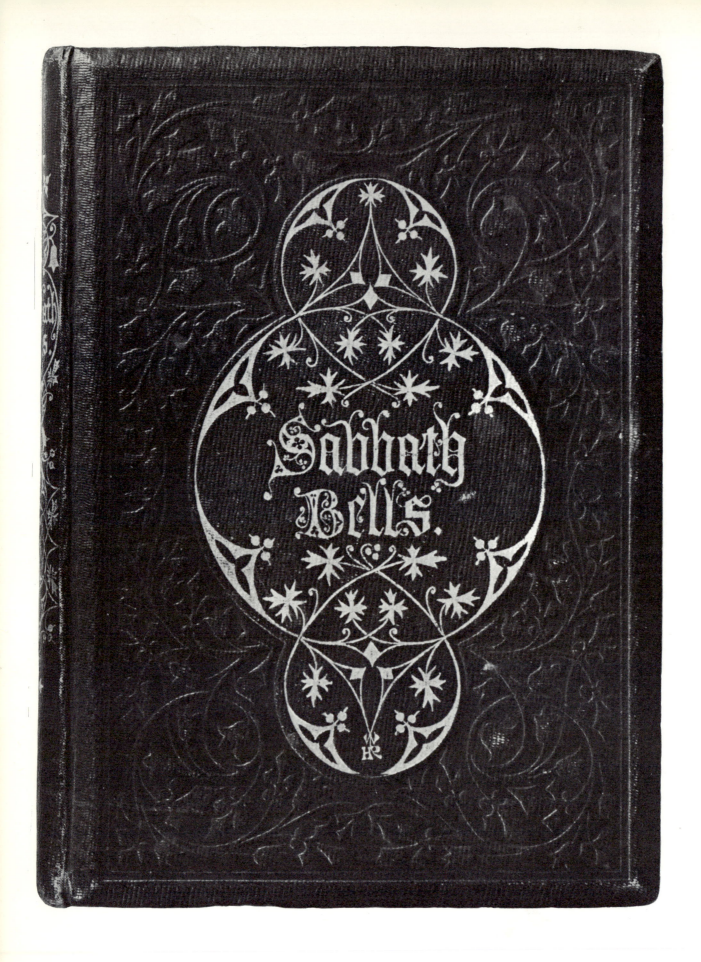

Sabbath Bells
Ed. Joseph Cundall, ill. B. Foster
Bell & Daldy, 1856
232 × 165 mm

Blue cloth blocked in gold and blind
on front and spine, bevelled boards.
Signed WHR. Bound by Bone &
Son.

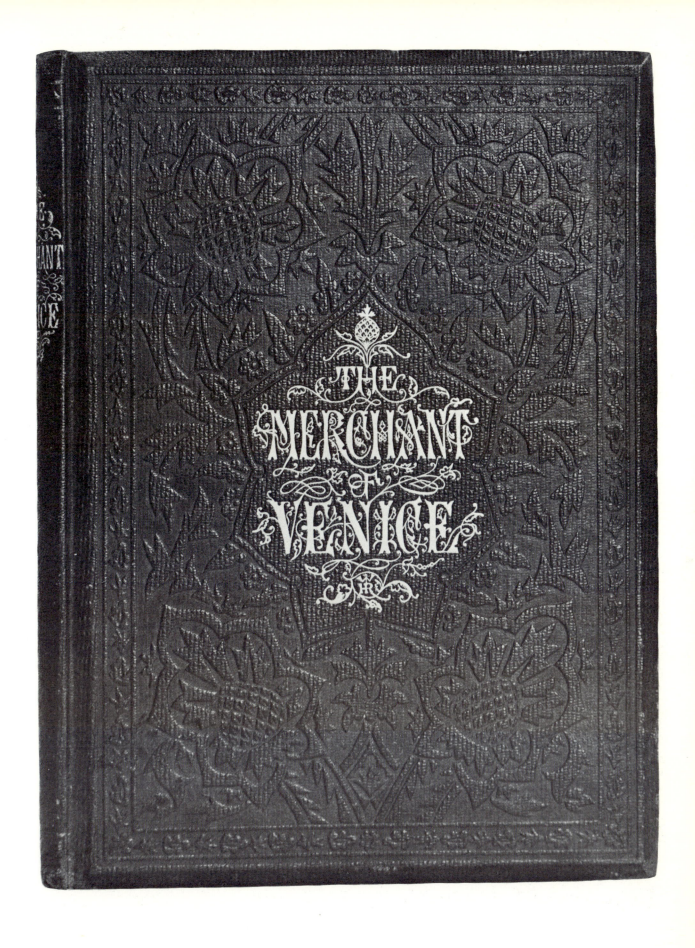

The Merchant of Venice
W. Shakespeare, ed. J. Cundall
Sampson Low, 1860
230 × 165 mm

Blue ribbed cloth blocked in gold and
blind on front and spine, bevelled
boards. Signed W.H.R.
Collection Fianach Lawry

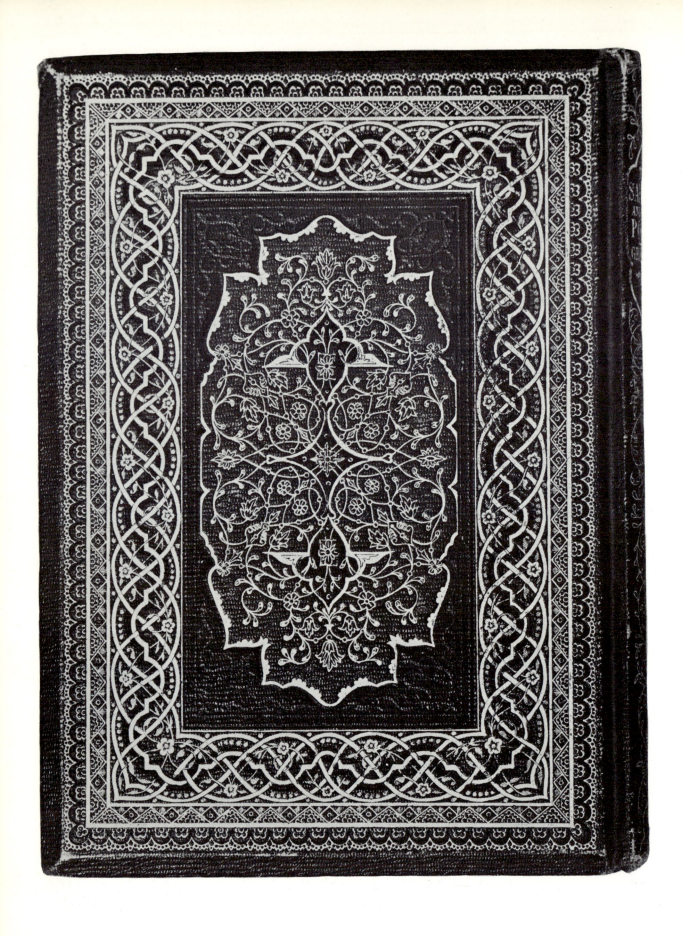

The Sabbath
James Graham, ill. B. Foster
Nisbet, 1857
212 × 150 mm

Blue ribbed cloth blocked in black
and gold, bevelled boards. Label:
Leighton Son & Hodge.
Collection Fianach Lawry

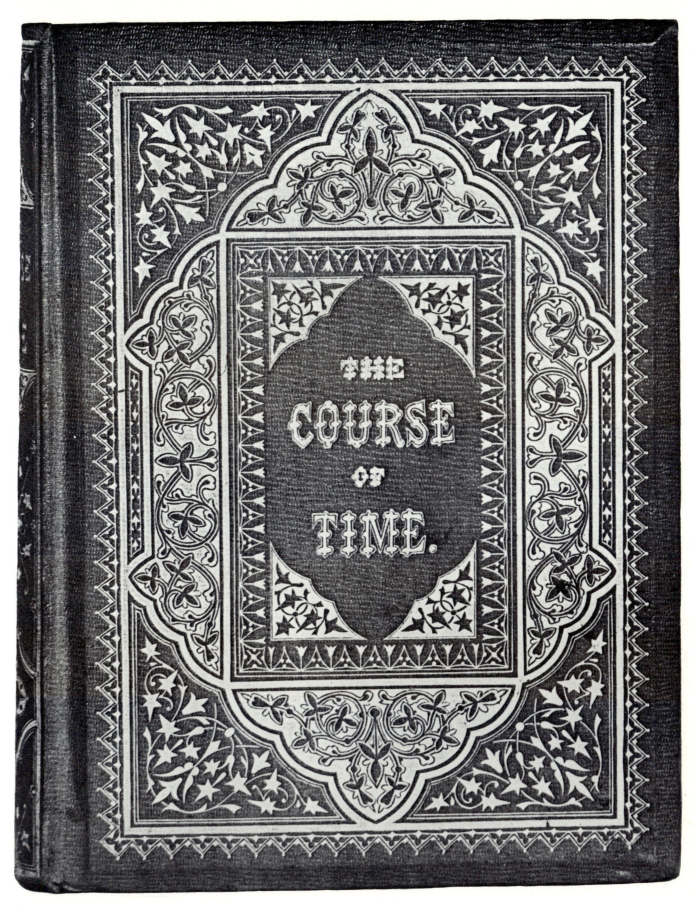

The Course of Time
Robert Pollok
Blackwood, 1857
229 × 162 mm

Orange cloth blocked in gold,
identical design on front and back,
bevelled boards. Signed JS (John
Sliegh). Label: Bound by Edmonds
& Remnants, London
Collection Fianach Lawry

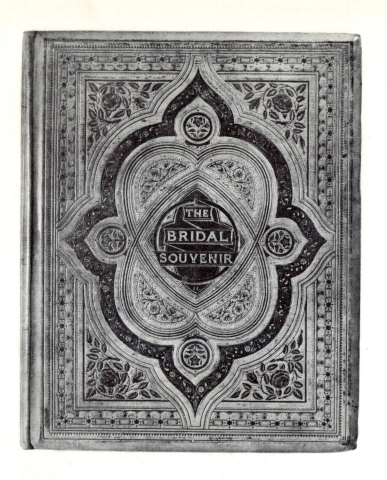

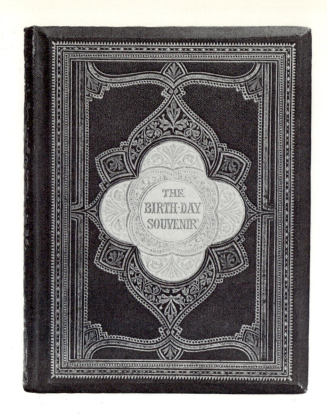

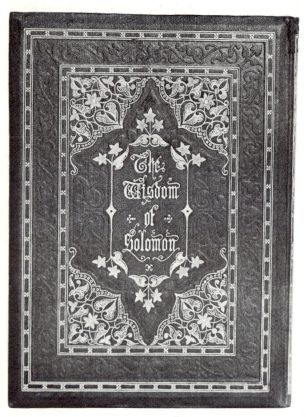

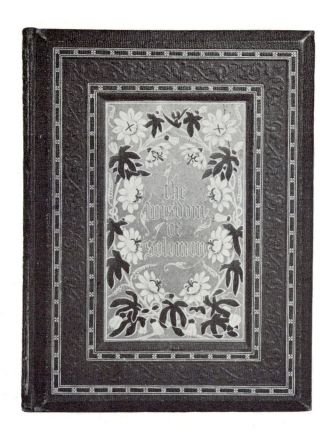

The Bridal Souvenir
Illum. Samuel Stanesby
Griffith & Farran n.d. (1857)
223 × 171 mm

White cloth with turquoise cut-out paper onlays blocked in gold, identical design front and back, blocked in gold only on spine, bevelled boards. Signed JL.

The Birthday Souvenir
Illum. S. Stanesby
Griffith & Farran, n.d. (c.1860)
187 × 137 mm

Green cloth with white cut-out paper onlays blocked in gold, identical design on front and back, blocked in gold only on spine, bevelled boards. Signed JL. Bound by W Bone & Son.
Collection Fianach Lawry

The Wisdom of Solomon
Illum. S. Stanesby
Griffith & Farran, n.d. (c.1861)
190 × 135 mm

Left
Red cloth blocked in gold and blind on front, back, and spine, bevelled boards.
Collection Fianach Lawry

Right
A variant binding on the same book. Purple cloth blocked in gold and blind, with paper panel chromolithographed in gold and colours in sunk panel, bevelled boards.
Collection Fianach Lawry

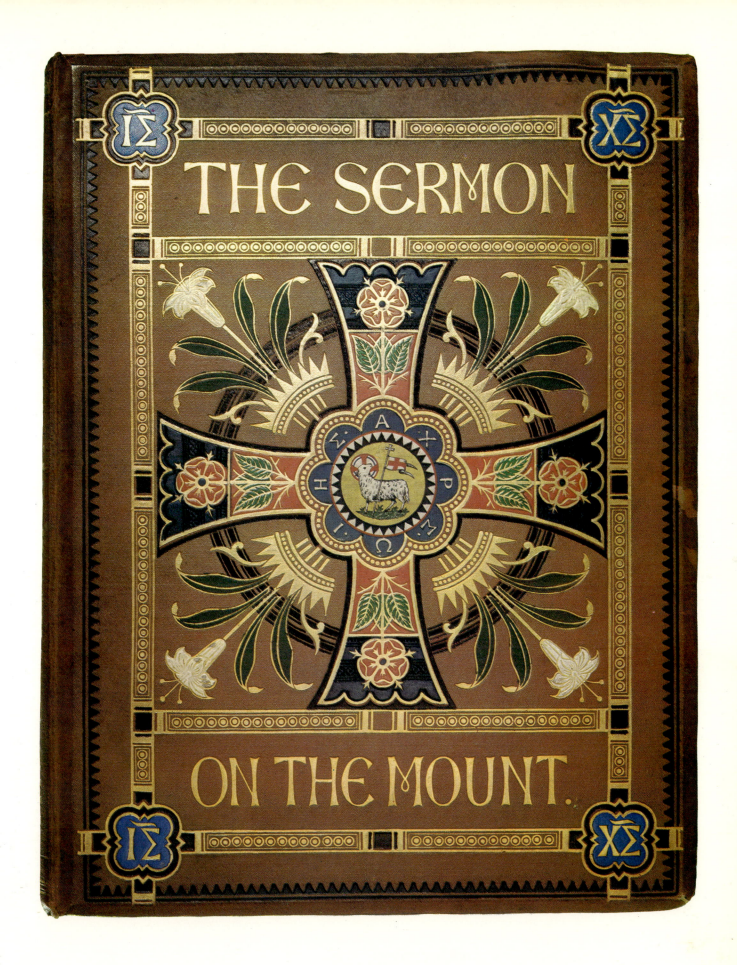

The Sermon on the Mount
Illuminated by W. and G. Audsley,
chromolithographed by W. R. Tymms
Day & Son, 1861
356 × 264 mm

Brown cloth with thirteen coloured and chromolithographed cut-out paper onlays, blocked in gold and black, and the leaves coloured green, bevelled boards; blocked in gold only on the spine and in blind on the back.

Scenes from The Winter's Tale
Illuminated by Owen Jones and
Henry Warren
Day & Son, n.d. (c.1866)
290 × 215 mm

Fawn morocco-grained cloth with
cut-out paper border only coloured
in orange and purple, blocked in gold,
identical design front and back,

blocked in gold only on spine,
bevelled boards.

The Winter's Tale is set in 'Sicilia'
and 'Bohemia', and Owen Jones's
decorations to the text, echoed in the
binding design, make much use of
the acanthus and other classical
motifs.
Collection Don Parkinson

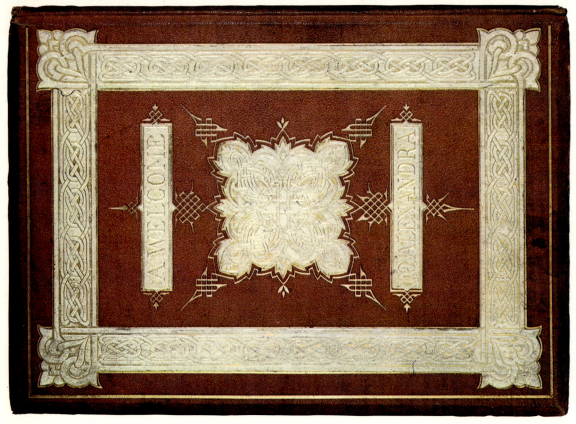

*A Welcome to Alexandra . . . from the
Poet Laureate*
Illuminated by Owen Jones
Day & Son, 1863
298 × 213 mm

Red morocco-grained cloth with
white paper onlays blocked in gold,
identical design front and back,
bevelled boards, blocked in gold only

on spine. This design by Owen Jones,
incorporating Celtic interlacing and
the Danish colours, was in honour of
the Danish Princess who married the
Prince of Wales in 1863 and became
Queen Alexandra.
Collection Fianach Lawry

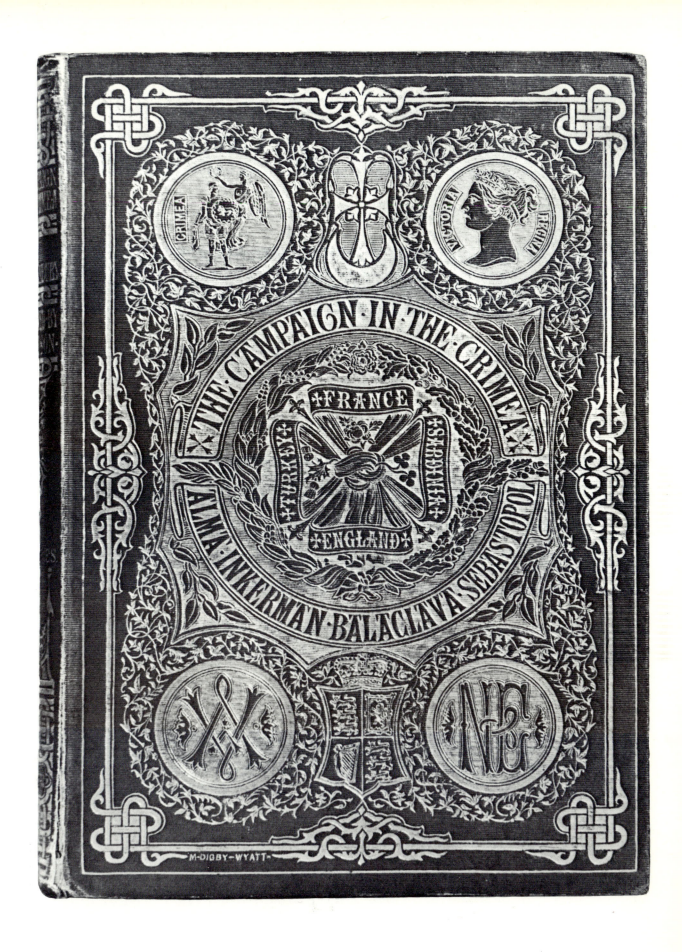

The Campaign in the Crimea, 2nd series
G. Brackenbury, ill. W. Simpson
P. & D. Colnaghi, 1856
256 × 171 mm

Blue fine-ribbed cloth blocked in gold on front and spine, in blind on back. Signed M. DIGBY WYATT. Label: Leighton Son & Hodge, Shoe Lane, London.

The Bouquet of Beauty
Blackwood, n.d. (*c.*1858)
264 × 183 mm

Red bead-grained cloth blocked in
gold on front, in blind on back.
Collection Fianach Lawry

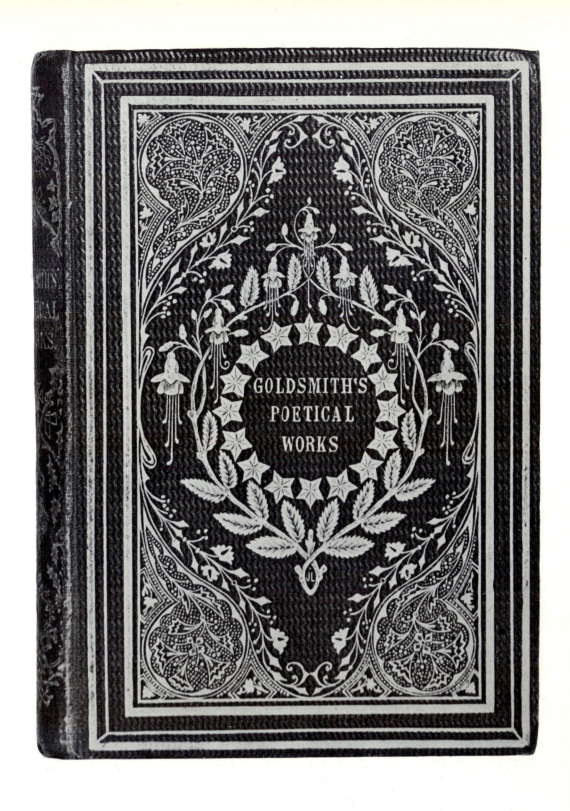

*The Poetical Works of Oliver Gold-
smith*
W. Kent, late D. Bogue, 1859
184 × 120 mm

Purple wavy grain cloth blocked in
gold on front and spine. Signed JL.
Collection Fianach Lawry

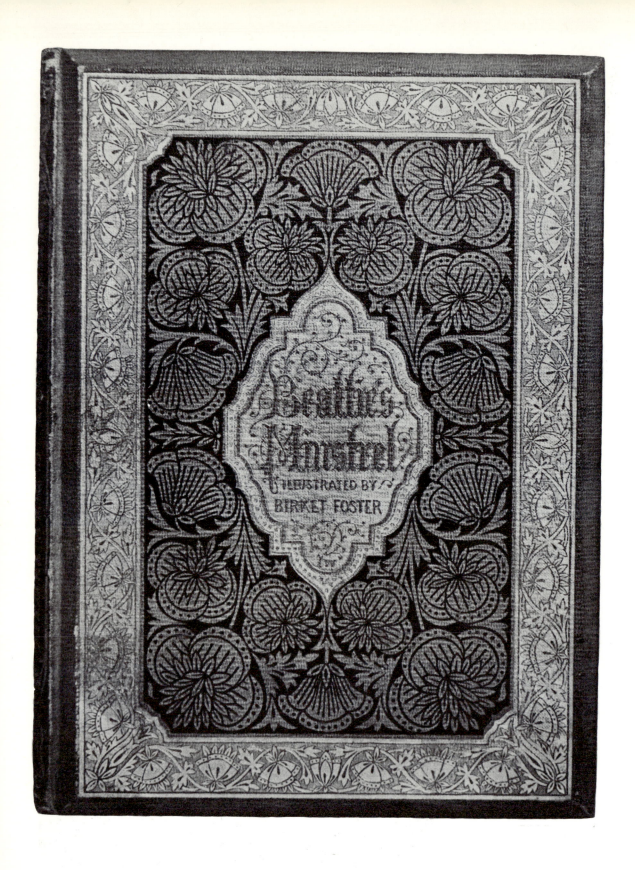

The Minstrel
James Beattie, ill. B. Foster
Routledge, 1858
206 × 146 mm

Blue cloth blocked in gold and black
on front and back, in gold only on
spine, bevelled boards. Signed A.W.
Collection Fianach Lawry

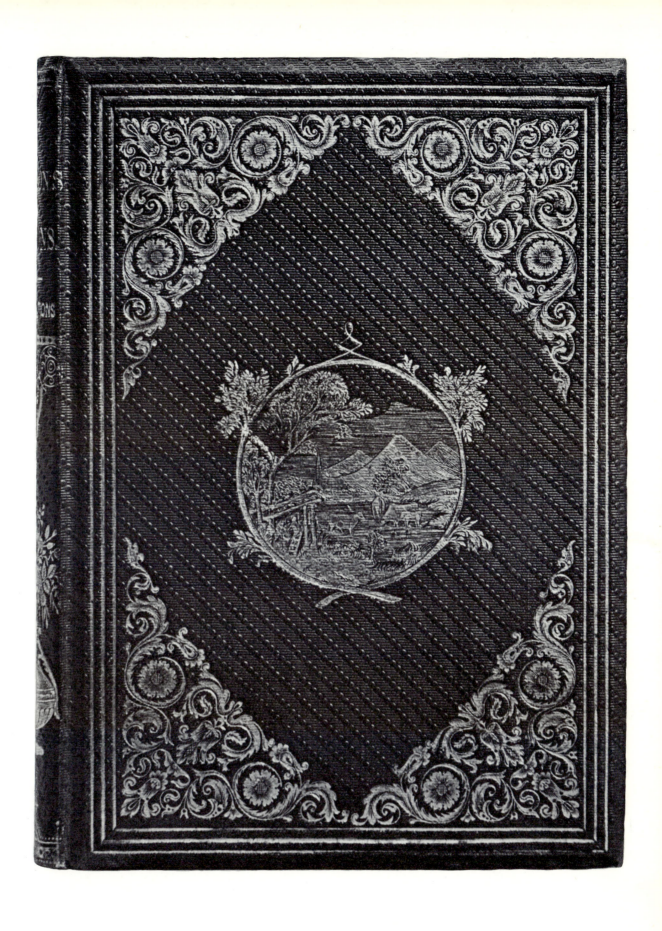

The Seasons
James Thomson
Nisbet, 1859
210 × 146 mm

Blue diagonally embossed cloth
blocked in gold on front and spine,
blind on back, bevelled boards.
Collection Fianach Lawry

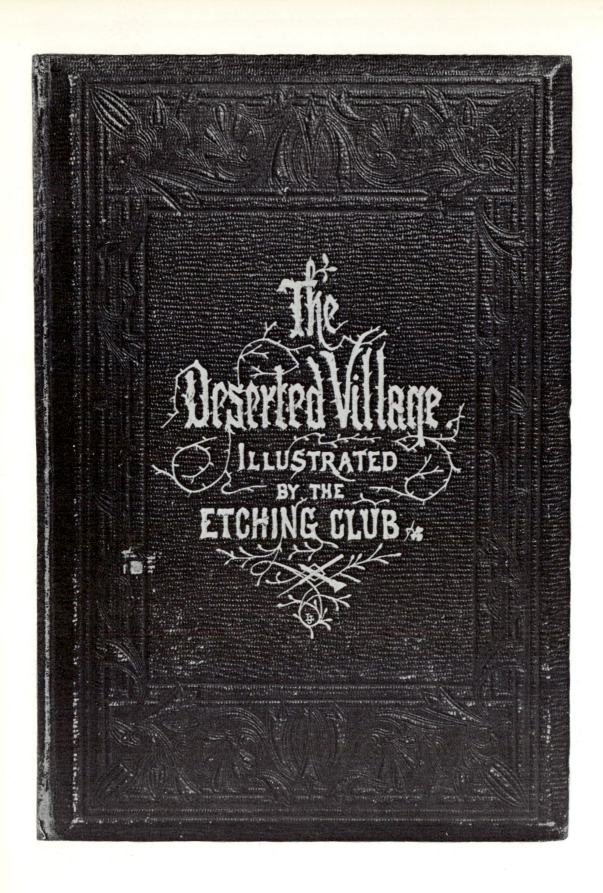

The Deserted Village
O. Goldsmith, ill. the Etching Club
Sampson Low for J. Cundall, 1855
205 × 133 mm

Blue leather-grained cloth in blind
and gold on front and spine, bevelled
boards. Signed JL.
Collection Fianach Lawry

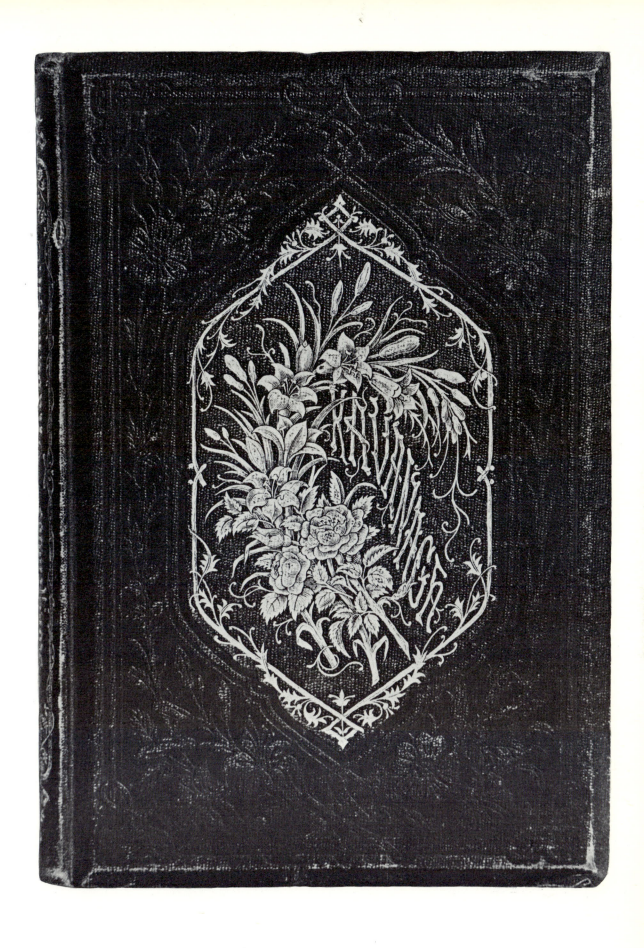

Kavanagh: a tale
H. W. Longfellow, ill. B. Foster
W. Kent, late D. Bogue, 1858
218 × 140 mm

Blue cloth blocked in blind and gold
on front and spine, bevelled boards.
Collection Fianach Lawry

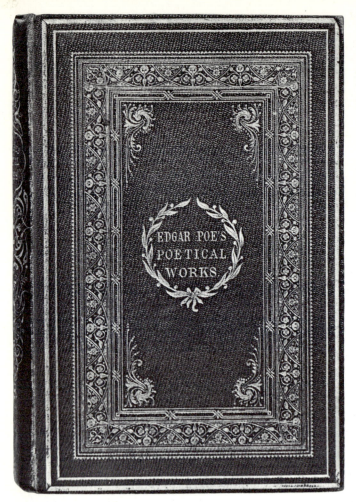

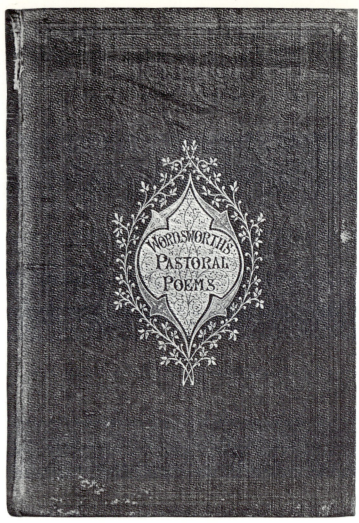

Poetical Works of E.A. Poe
Kent, 1859
187 × 124 mm

Blue grained cloth blocked in gold on
front and spine, blind on back.
Collection Fianach Lawry

Pastoral Poems
W. Wordsworth
Sampson Low for J. Cundall, 1860
202 × 132 mm

Magenta ripple-grained cloth blocked
in blind and gold on front and spine.
Bound by Bone & Son.
Collection Fianach Lawry

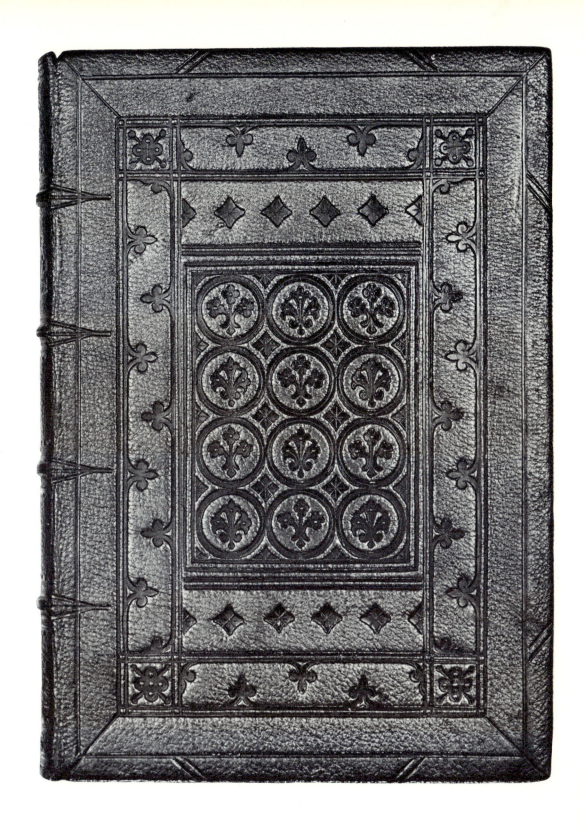

The Wife's Manual, etc., 3rd edition
Rev. W. Calvert
Longman, 1861
196 × 132 mm

Brown morocco blocked in dark
brown. Bound by Edmonds &
Remnants.
Collection R. de Beaumont

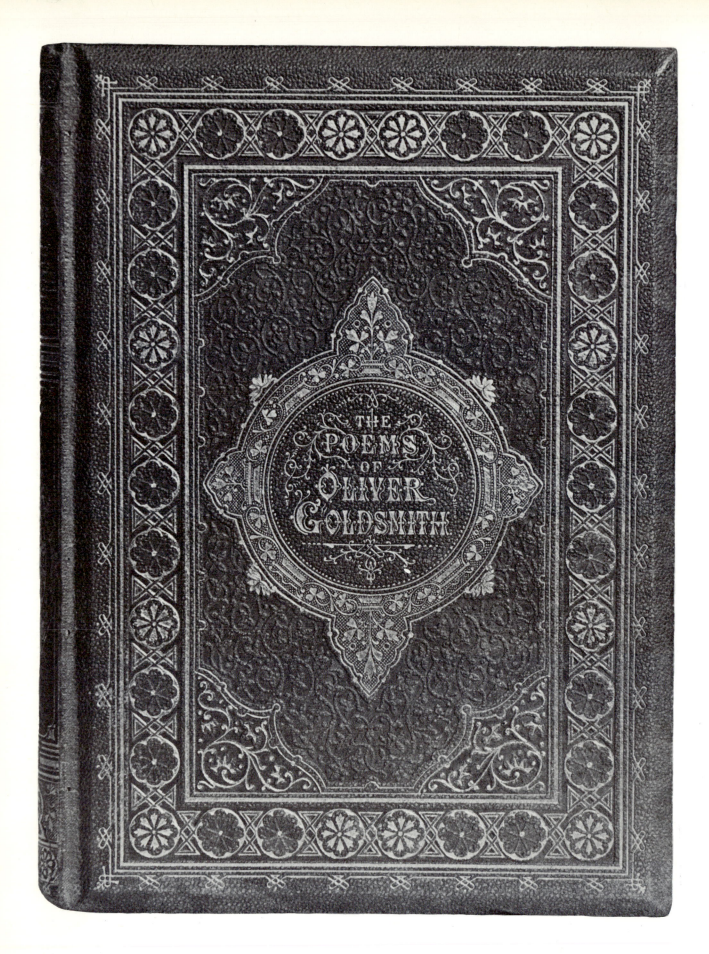

The Poems of Oliver Goldsmith
Ed. R. A. Willmott, ill. B. Foster and
  H. N. Humphreys
Routledge, 1860
232 × 160 mm

Red cloth blocked in gold and blind
on front, spine, and back, bevelled
boards.
Collection R. de Beaumont

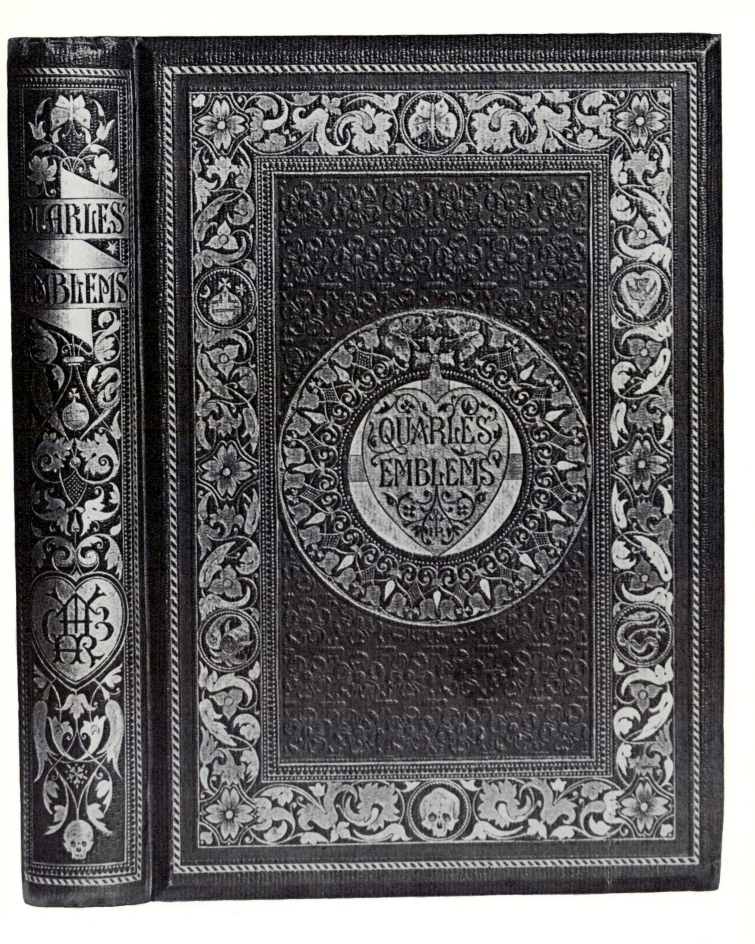

Quarles' Emblems
Ill. Charles Bennett and W. Harry
  Rogers
Nisbet, 1861
228×155 mm

Blue cloth blocked in gold and blind
on front, spine and back, bevelled
boards. Signed W.H.R.
Collection R. de Beaumont

The Tempest
W. Shakespeare, ill. G. Doré,
 B. Foster *et al.*
Bell & Daldy, n.d. (*c.*1860)
254 × 184 mm

Blue grained cloth blocked in gold
and blind on front and spine. Label:
Bone & Son, 76 Fleet Street, London

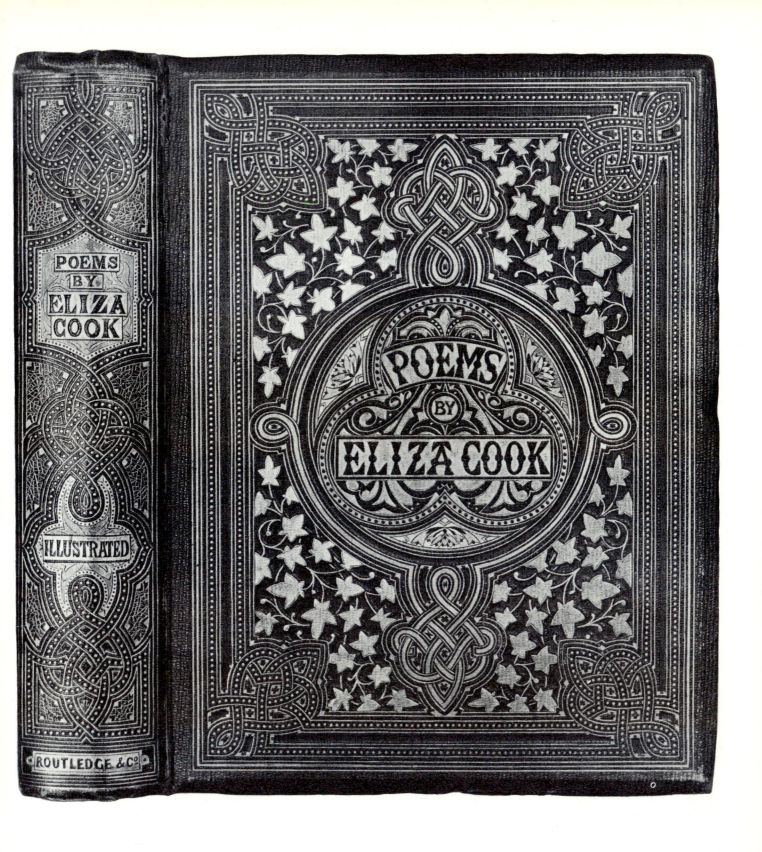

Poems
Eliza Cook
Routledge, 1861
232 × 168 mm

Violet blue morocco-grained cloth,
blocked in gold and blind on front,
in gold only on spine, bevelled
boards. Signed JL. Label: Edmonds
& Remnants, London.
Collection Fianach Lawry

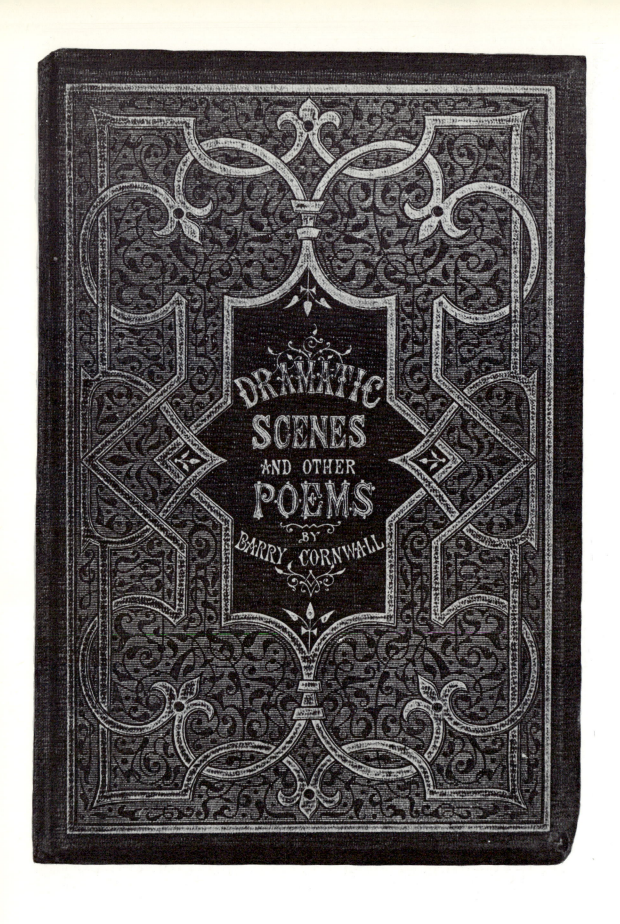

Dramatic Scenes, with other Poems
Barry Cornwall
Chapman & Hall, 1857
208 × 136 mm

Green morocco-grained cloth blocked
in gold on front and spine, bevelled
boards.
Collection Fianach Lawry

86

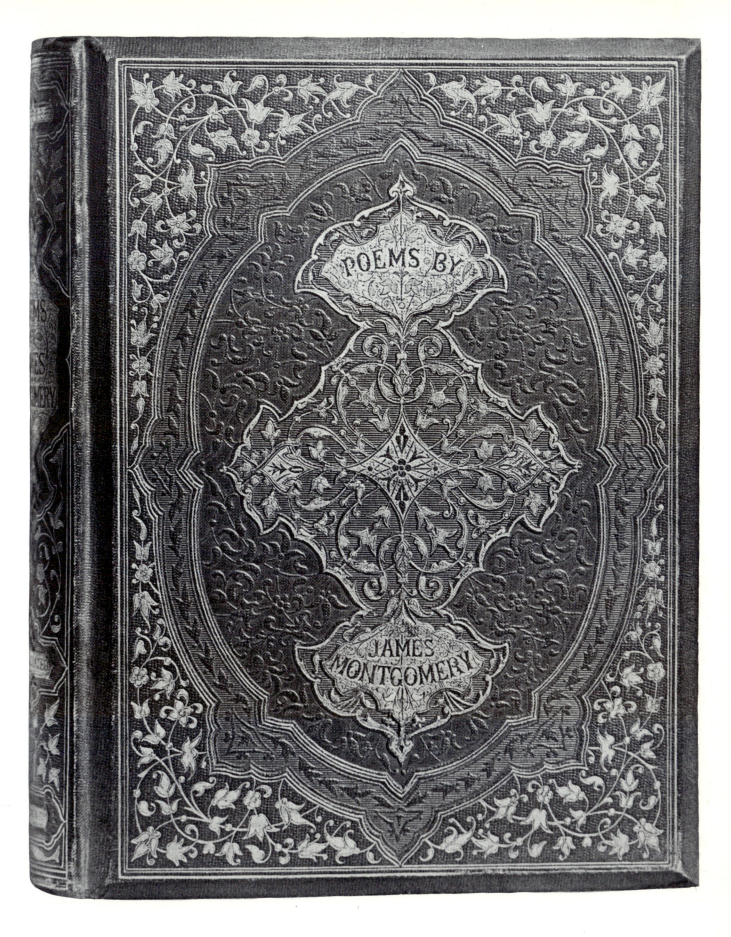

Poems
James Montgomery, ed. R. A. Will-
    mott
Routledge, 1860
229 × 165 mm

Blue cloth blocked in gold and blind
on front, spine and back, with deep
embossing and bevelled boards.
Bound by Leighton Son & Hodge.
Collection Fianach Lawry

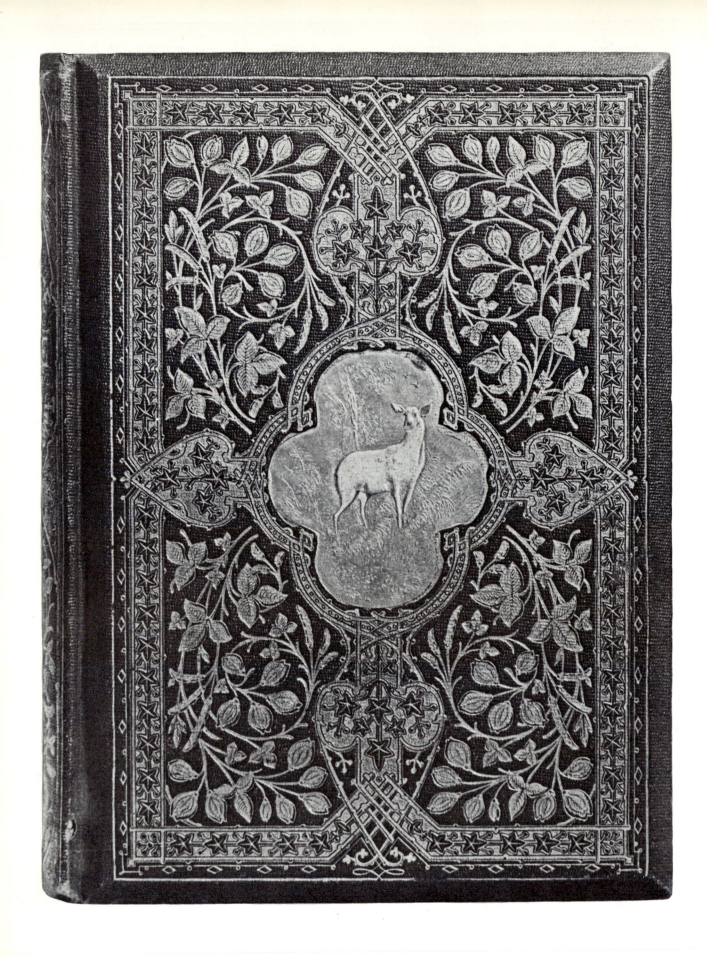

The White Doe of Rylstone
W. Wordsworth
Longman, 1859
225 × 159 mm

Dark red grained cloth with white
onlay on front and back, blocked in
gold, spine blocked in gold, bevelled
boards.
Collection Fianach Lawry

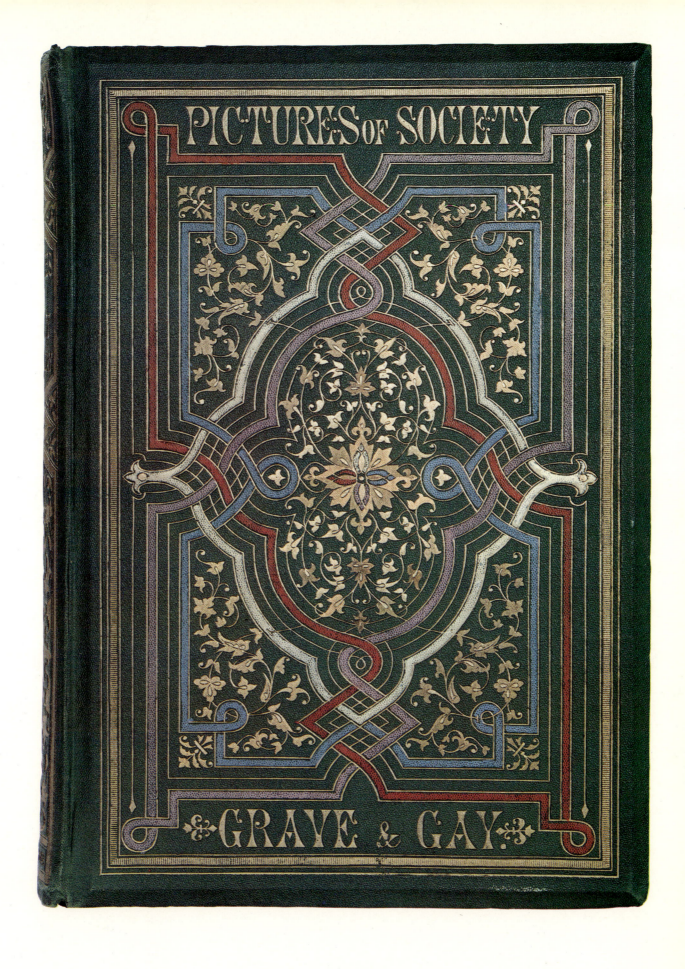

Pictures of Society Grave and Gay
Sampson Low, 1866
257 × 170 mm

Green cloth with design coloured in red, mauve, blue, and white and blocked in gold, the gold block repeated on the back, without colouring, spine blocked in gold only, bevelled boards.

On this remarkable cover, alas unsigned, the colours appear to have been applied to the cloth by brush and stencil.
Collection R. de Beaumont

The Life of Man
Ill. John Leighton
Longmans, 1866
286 × 220 mm

Green cloth with red paper mandorla onlay. Signed JL. Blocked in gold and black, identical design on front and back, spine blocked in gold and black, bevelled boards. Label: Edmonds and Remnants.

Nearly all the books illustrated in *Victorian Publishers' Bookbindings* have all edges gilt; this one has a refinement, in that while top and bottom edges are gilt, the fore-edge is gilt and red stripes.

Collection C. Dobson

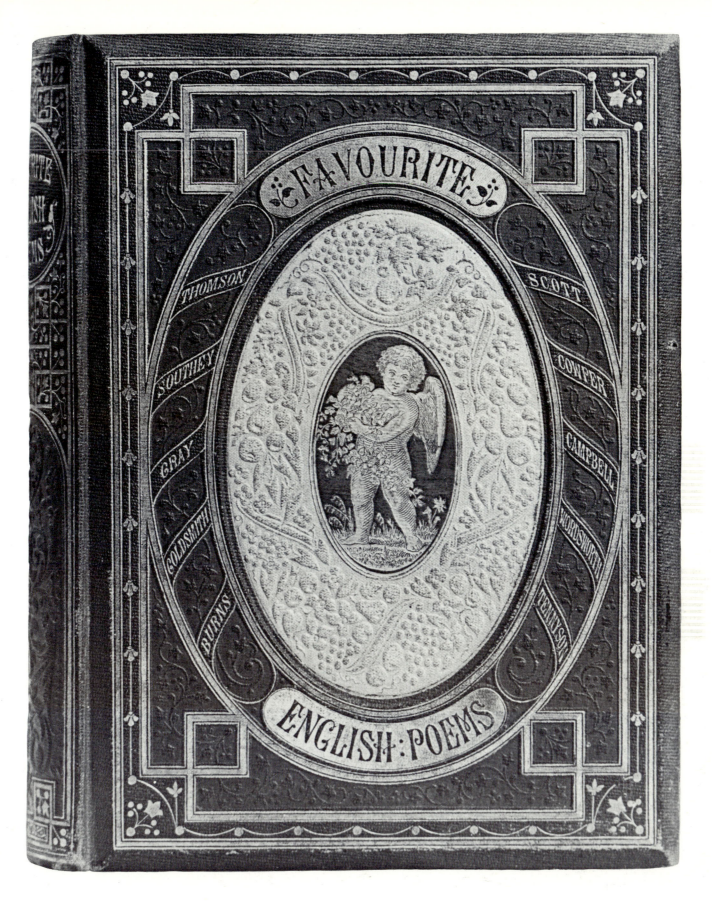

Favourite English Poems of Modern Times
Ed. Joseph Cundall
Sampson Low, 1862
229 × 165 mm

Blue cloth with white and blue oval paper onlays, blocked in gold and blind, with deep embossing on front and back and in gold and blind on spine, bevelled boards. Signed RD (Robert Dudley). Bound by Leighton Son & Hodge
Collection Fianach Lawry

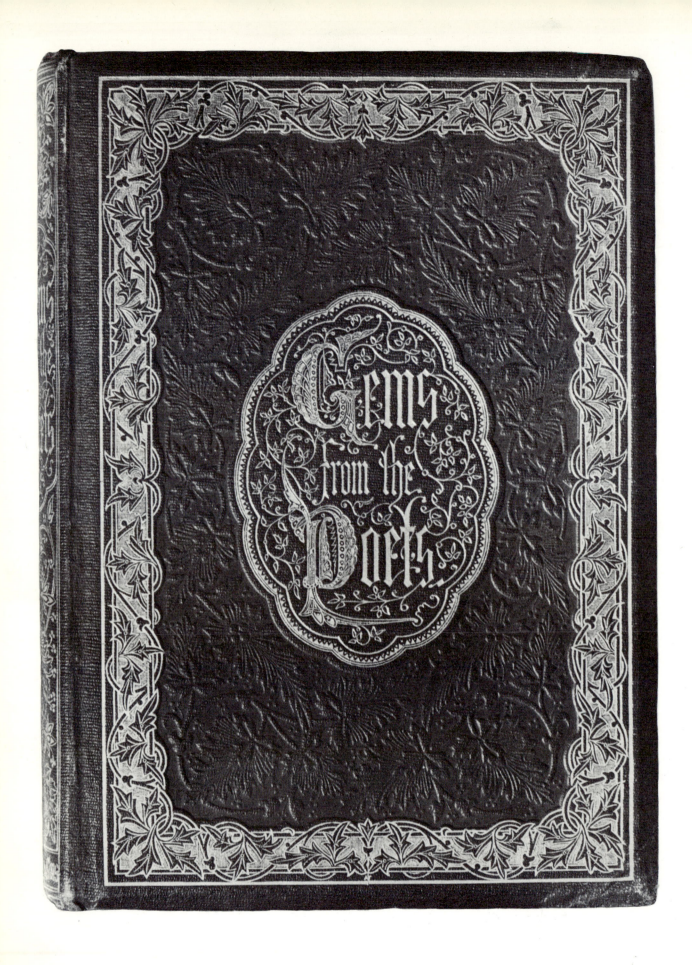

Gems from the Poets
Ill. A. F. Lydon
Groombridge, n.d. (*c.*1860)
256 × 178 mm

Blue cloth blocked in gold and blind
on front, spine, and back, bevelled
boards. Signed AW.

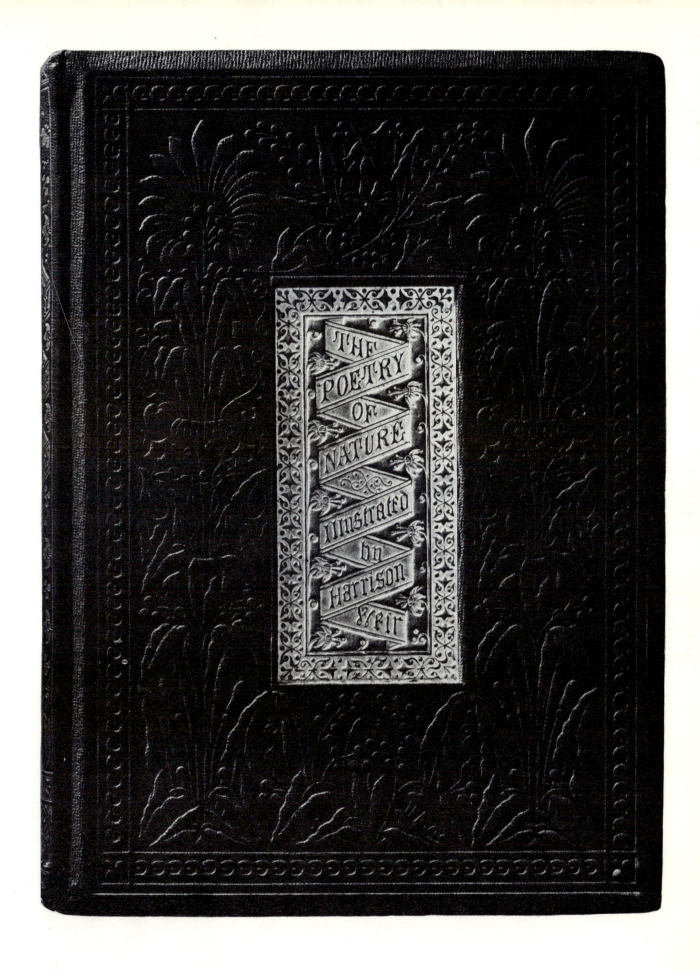

The Poetry of Nature
Harrison Weir
Sampson Low, 1861
228 × 158 mm

Mauve cloth with white paper onlay, blocked in gold and blind, identical design front and back, spine blocked in gold, bevelled boards.

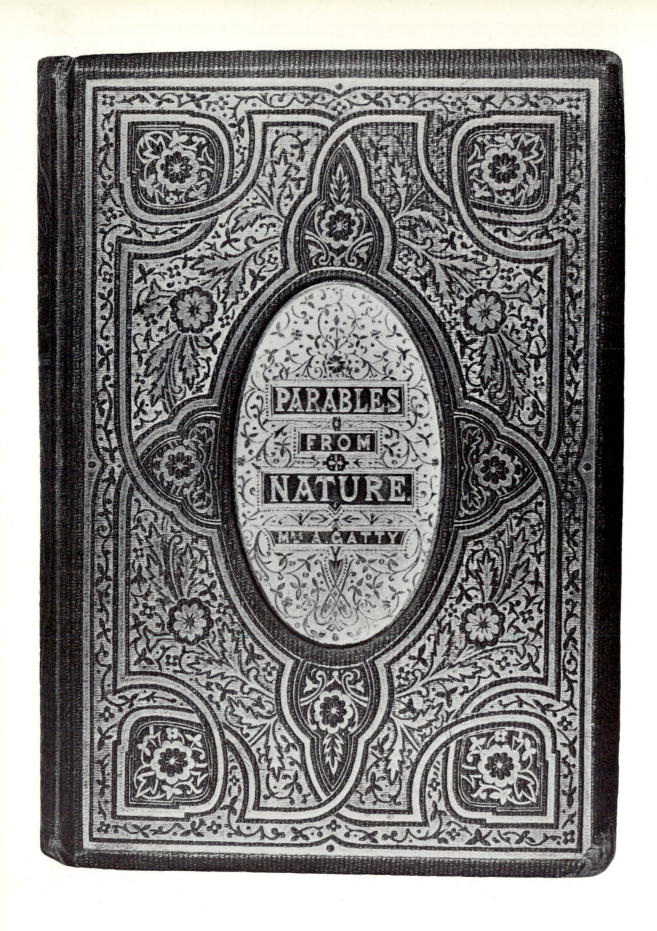

Parables from Nature
Mrs A. Gatty
Bell & Daldy, 1861
205 × 140 mm

Blue cloth with white paper onlay in
sunk oval panel, blocked in gold,
bevelled boards.

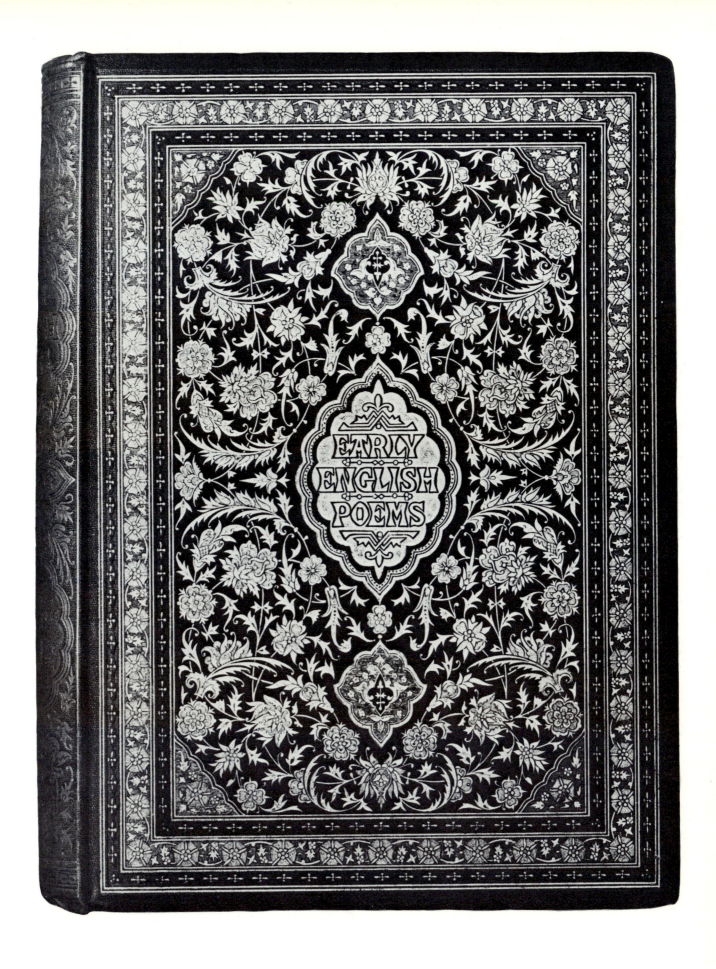

Early English Poems
Ed. Joseph Cundall
Sampson Low, 1863
228 × 158 mm

Purple cloth blocked in gold and blind on front and spine, and blind on back, bevelled boards. Signed A.W. Label: W. Bone & Son.

Household Song: collection of lyrical pieces
Ill. B. Foster, H. Weir *et al.*
Kent, 1861
215 × 158 mm

Red bead grain cloth blocked in gold
on front and spine, bevelled boards.
Collection Fianach Lawry

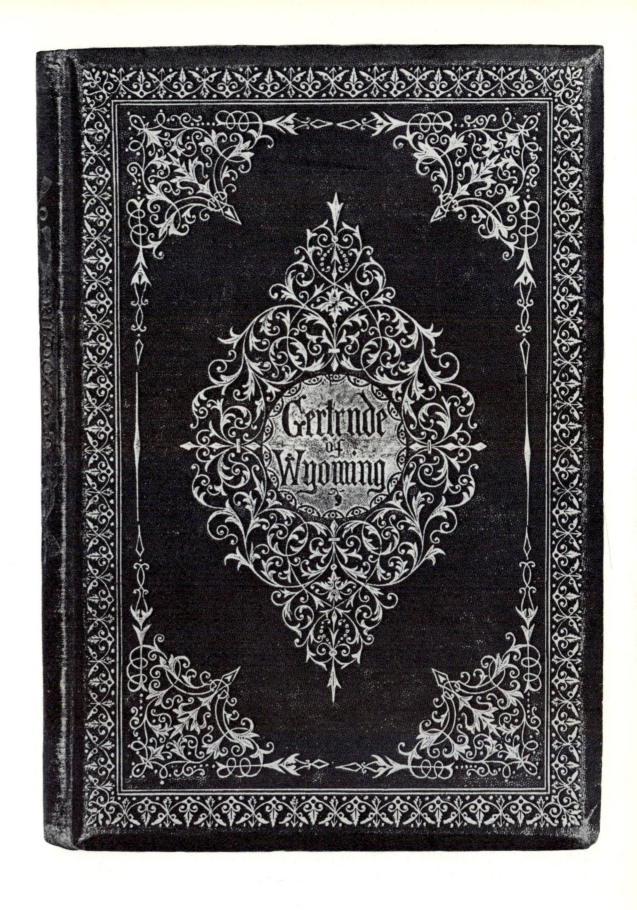

Gertrude of Wyoming
T. Campbell
Routledge, 1862
210 × 140 mm

Green fine-grained cloth blocked in
gold on front and spine.
Collection Fianach Lawry

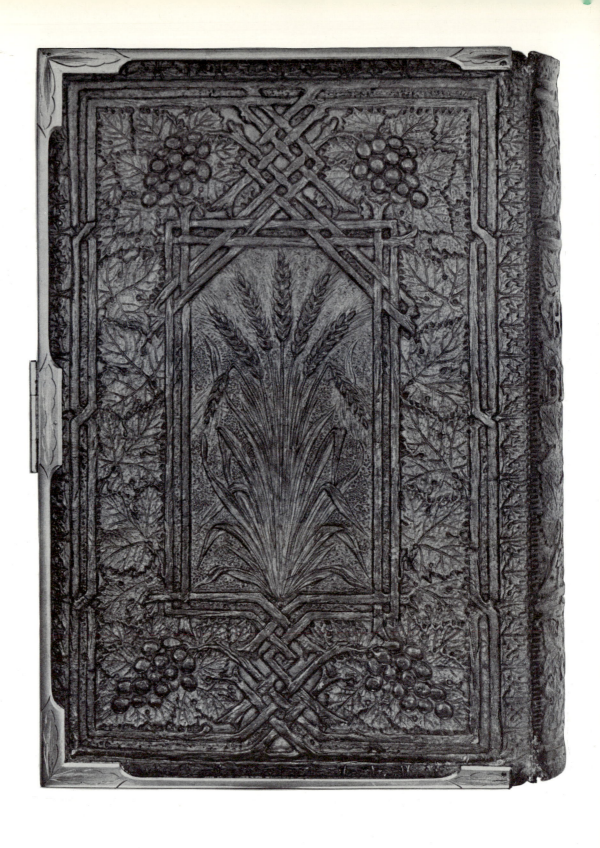

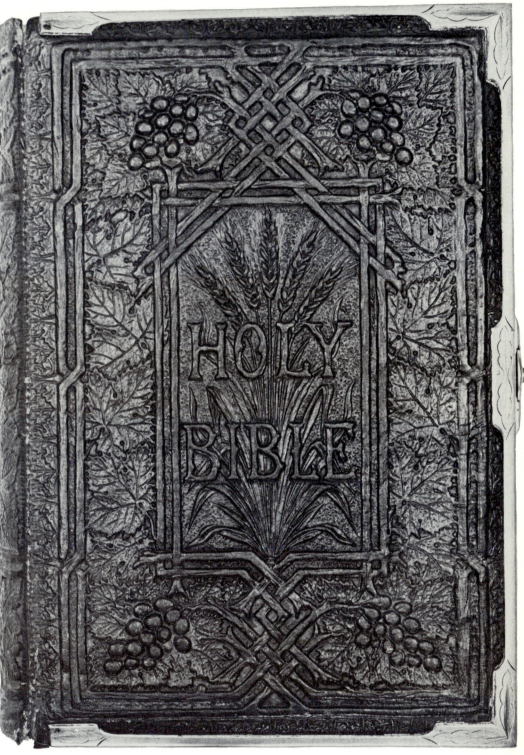

The Holy Bible
Ward & Lock, 1862
229 × 150 mm

Brown *relievo* leather with brass edging and clasp. Designed by Owen Jones. The design is in strong relief.
Collection R. de Beaumont

Pictures of English Landscape
B. Foster
Routledge, 1862
263 × 175 mm

Blue cloth blocked in gold on sides,
identical design front and back, and
on spine, bevelled boards. Designed
by Owen Jones.

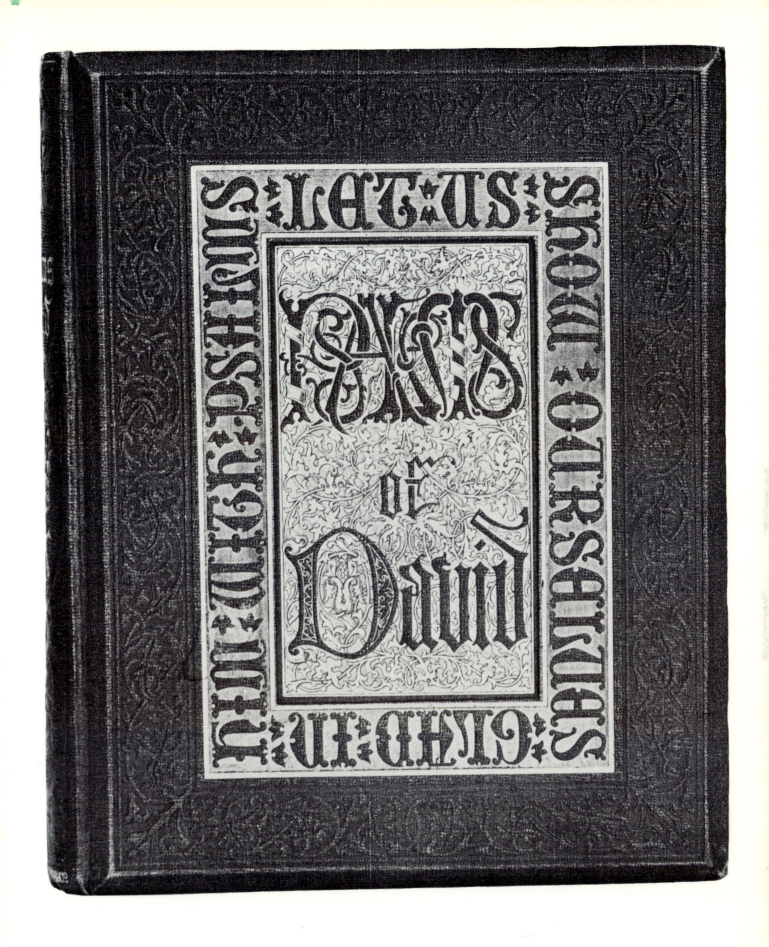

The Psalms of David
Ill. John Franklin, engraved by
   W. J. Linton
Sampson Low, 1862
240 × 185 mm

Blue cloth blocked in gold and blind on front, back and spine. Label: Bound by Bone & Son, 76 Fleet Street, London.
  A superb design based on the decorative use of lettering – but who designed it?
Collection R. de Beaumont

Paradise and the Peri
T. Moore, illum. Owen Jones
Day & Son, n.d. (*c.*1860)
336 × 245 mm

Dark yellow cloth blocked in gold
and blind on front and back, and in
gold on spine, bevelled boards.
Designed by Owen Jones.
Collection Fianach Lawry

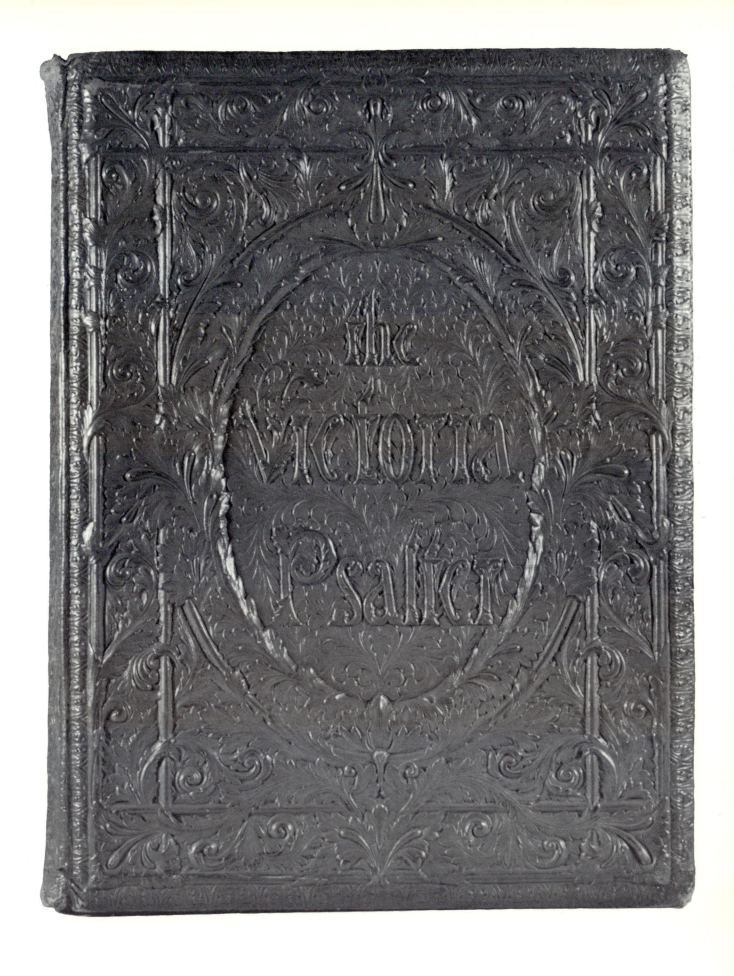

The Victoria Psalter
Illum. Owen Jones
Day & Son, 1861
419 × 311 mm

Brown *relievo* leather, designed by
Owen Jones, with different designs
in deep relief on front and back.

Ruined Abbeys and Castles of Great Britain
William & Mary Howitt, ill. with
  photographs by Bedford, Fenton
  et al.
A. W. Bennett, 1862
228 × 165 mm

Purple cloth with circular photograph onlay front and back, blocked
in gold and blind on front and back,
in gold only on spine, bevelled
boards. The design, is probably by
John Leighton, but is unsigned.

The Book of the Thames
Mr & Mrs S. C. Hall, ill. with
  photographs
Alfred W. Bennett, 1867
228 × 158 mm

Blue cloth blocked in gold, with
circular photo onlays (identical front
and back), blocked in gold only on
spine. The design looks as if it must
be by John Leighton, but is unsigned.

Windsor, etc.
Rev. John Stoughton
Ward, 1862
190 × 120 mm

Brown cloth printed with black
simulation of wood grain and
blocked in gold on front and spine.
Label: Westleys & Co.
Collection R. de Beaumont

The White Doe of Rylstone
W. Wordsworth
Bell & Daldy, 1867
190 × 137 mm

Front and back of papier mâché
simulating green malachite, blocked
in gold. Spine in green leather
blocked in gold.
Collection R. de Beaumont

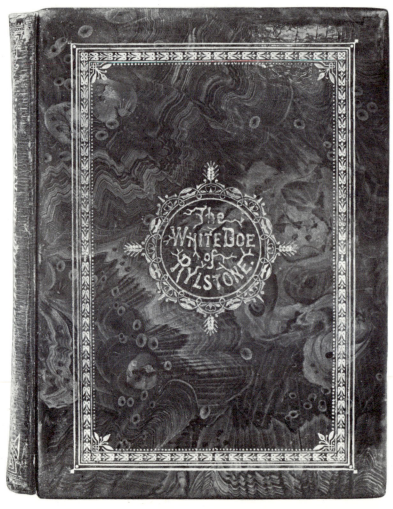

Poetry of the Year
Ed. Joseph Cundall
C. Griffin, n.d. (*c.*1867)
246 × 187 mm

Blue cloth blocked in gold and blind, with oval chromolithographed paper onlay, the same design on front and back but different chromolithograph on back, spine blocked in gold only,

bevelled boards.

The book is illustrated with pasted-down chromolithographs, probably by Vincent Brooks, whose name is on the chromolithographed title page. This was drawn by Albert Warren, who may therefore have also designed the binding, although the designs are totally dissimilar.
Collection Don Parkinson

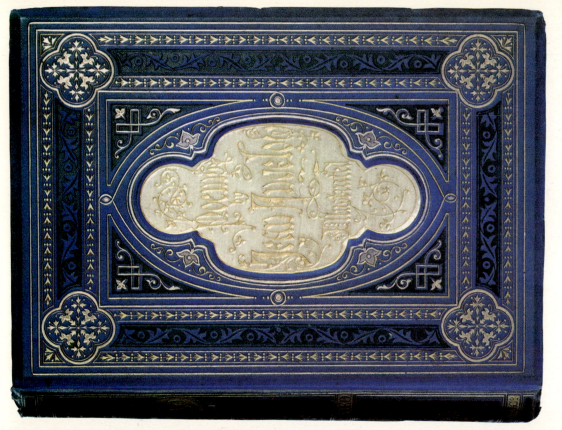

Poems
Jean Ingelow
Longmans, 1867
237 × 168 mm

Blue cloth, blocked in blind, with white cut-out paper onlay, the whole

blocked in gold and black, identical design front and back, spine blocked in gold and black, bevelled boards. This was also a Dalziel gift book, with illustrations by various artists.
Collection C. Dobson

The Spirit of Praise
F. Warne, n.d. (c.1867)
255 × 180 mm

Purple cloth blocked in blind, with turquoise cut-out paper onlay, the whole blocked in gold, identical

design front and back, spine blocked in gold and blind, bevelled boards. Label: Bound by W. Bone & Son, 76 Fleet Street, London E.C. This was a Dalziel gift book, printed in red and black throughout.
Collection C. Dobson

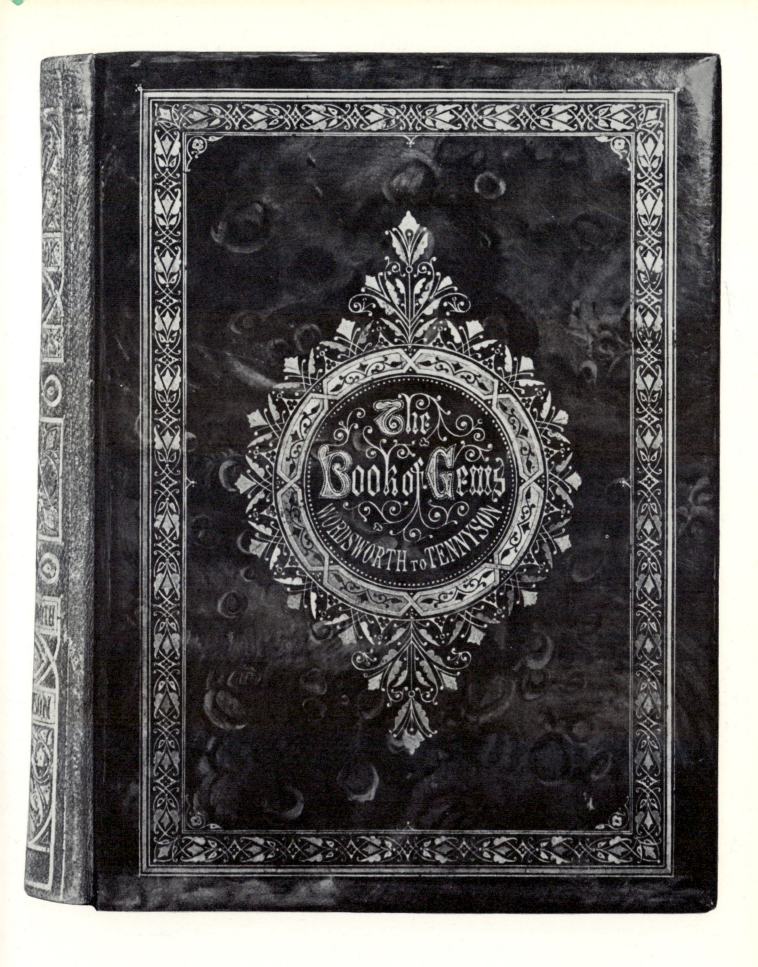

The Book of Gems
Ed. S. C. Hall
Bell & Daldy, 1871
226 × 164 mm

Imitation tortoiseshell (same design on front and back) sides, blocked in gold, spine blocked in gold on leather.
Collection C. Dobson

The Lake Country
E. Lynn Linton, ill. W. J. Linton
Smith, Elder, 1864
248 × 171 mm

Blue pebble-grained cloth blocked
in gold and blind on front, back and
spine, bevelled boards. Signed JL.
Collection Fianach Lawry

Robinson Crusoe
D. Defoe, ill. J. D. Watson
Routledge, 1864
235 × 168 mm

A Dalziel gift book. Blue cloth
blocked in gold and blind on sides.
identical design front and back, and
on spine, bevelled boards. Signed JL.
Bound by Leighton Son & Hodge.

The Church's Floral Kalandar
Illum. W. R. Tymms
Day & Son, n.d. inscribed 1861
245 × 193 mm

Blue cloth blocked in gold and blind
on front, spine, and back. In its
original state (this is a worn copy)
with the frieze of lettering round the
edges, this must have looked
magnificent, and looks as if it must
have been designed by John Leighton
although it is unsigned.
Collection Fianach Lawry

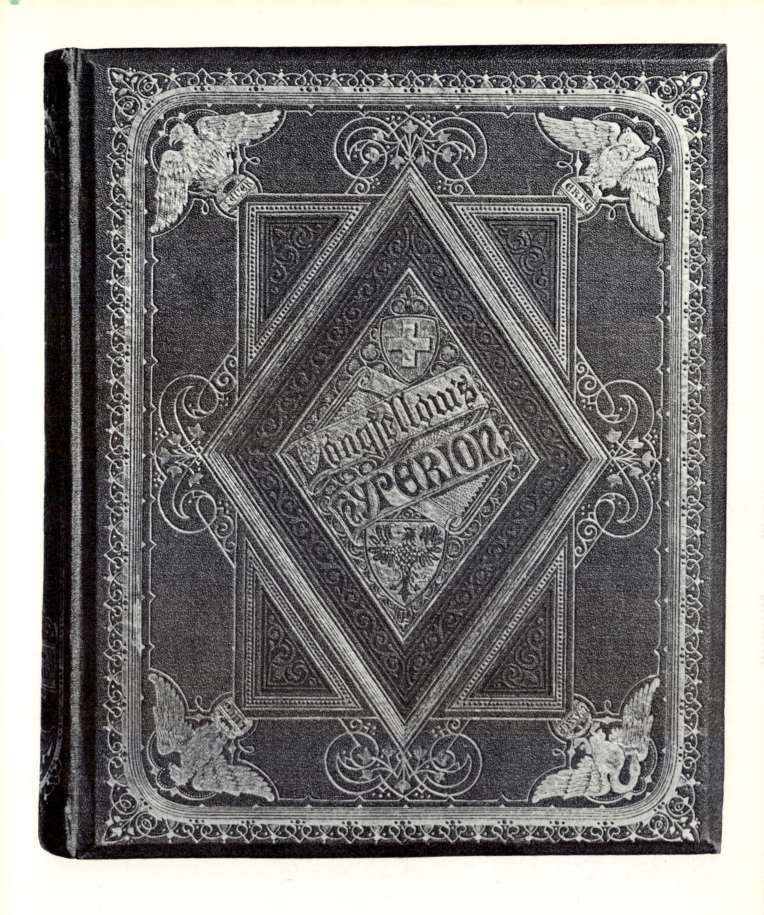

Hyperion
H. W. Longfellow, with twenty-four photographs by Francis Frith
Alfred W. Bennett, 1865
235 × 182 mm

Red cloth blocked in gold and blind on front, spine, and back, bevelled boards. Signed JL. Bound by Westleys.
Collection R. de Beaumont

A Chronicle of England
James E. Doyle
Longman, 1864
276 × 205 mm

Dark red cloth blocked in gold and
blind on front, spine, and back,
bevelled boards. Signed JL.
Collection R. de Beaumont

Picturesque Views of Seats, etc. . . in Great Britain & Ireland 6 volumes
Rev. F. O. Morris, ill. A. F. Lydon
W. Mackenzie, Edinburgh, n.d. (*c.* 1860s)
280 × 216 mm

Brown cloth blocked in gold and black and blind on front and spine, in blind on back, bevelled boards. Signed JL.

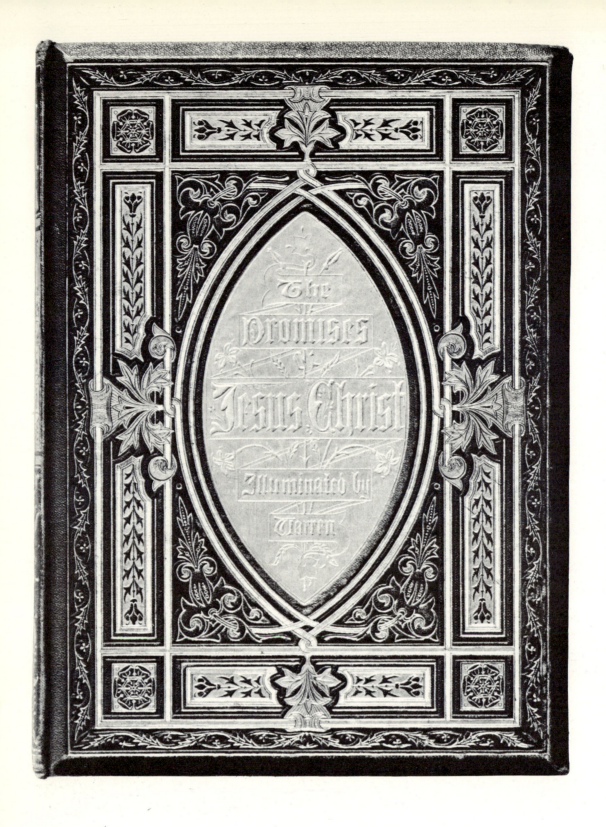

The Promises of Jesus Christ
Ill. Albert Warren
Day & Son, 1866
206 × 146 mm

Red cloth with white paper mandorla
onlay, bloked in gold and blind,
bevelled boards, signed AW (Albert
Warren)

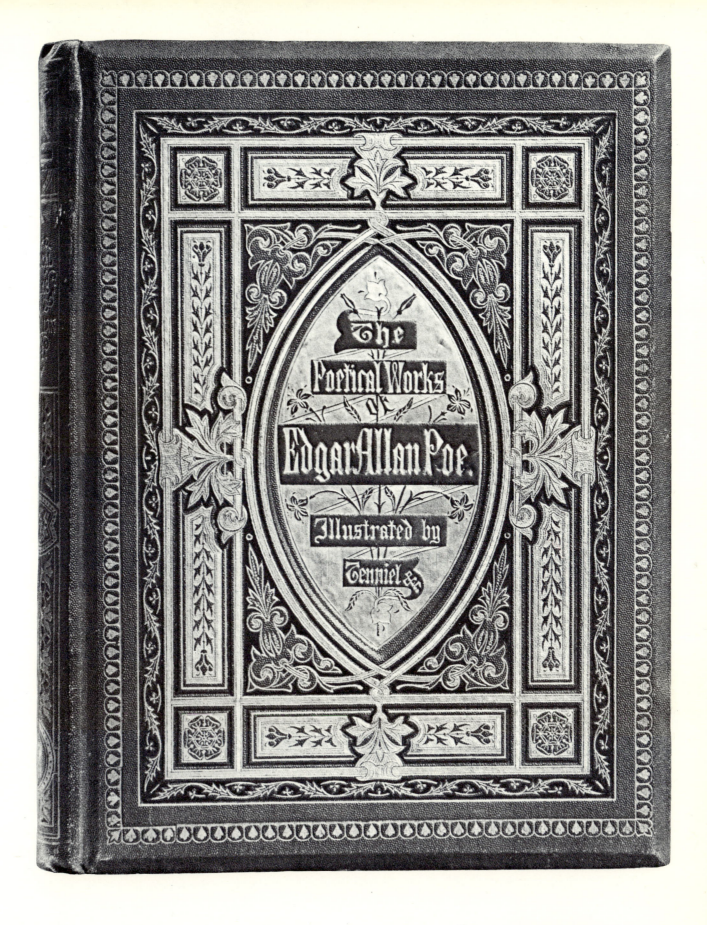

The Poetical Works of E. A. Poe
Ed. Joseph Cundall
Ward, Lock & Tyler, n.d. (*c.*1867)
235 × 165 mm

Green cloth with red paper mandorla
onlay, with deep embossing, blocked
in gold on front; blocked in gold and
black on spine, in blind on back,
bevelled boards. The block designed
for the previous book (facing) has
been here re-used on a larger book,
within a new border.

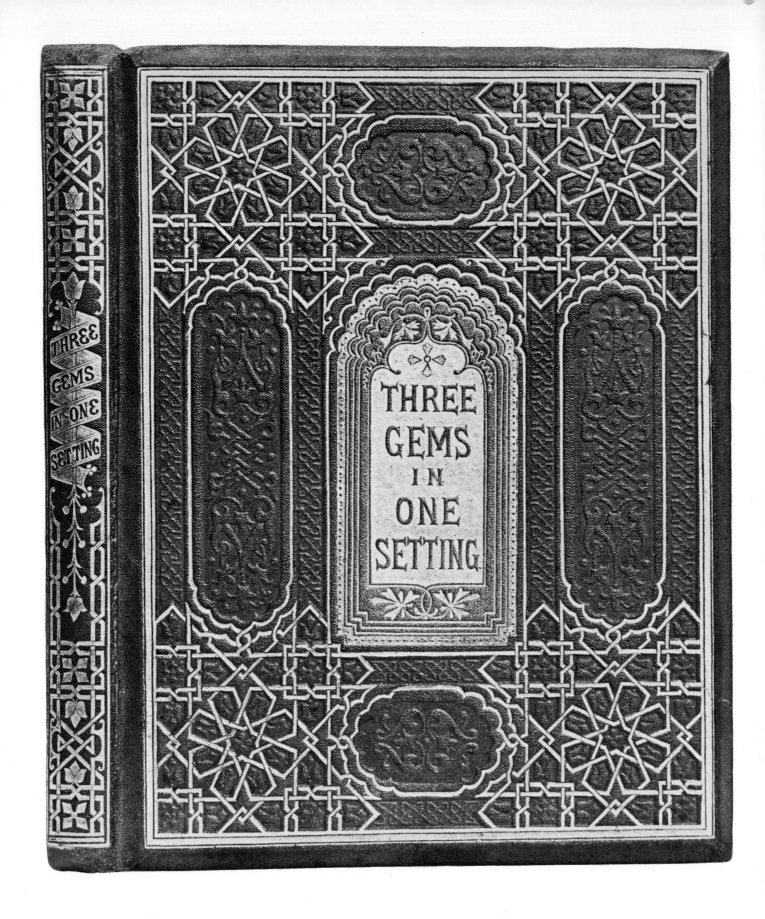

Three Gems in One Setting
A. L. Bond
Ward, Lock & Tyler, n.d. (*c.*1860)
216 × 165 mm

Blue cloth (or red cloth) with red
paper onlay on front and deep
embossed panels, blocked in gold
and blind on front, in gold on spine,
and blind on back.
Collection Fianach Lawry

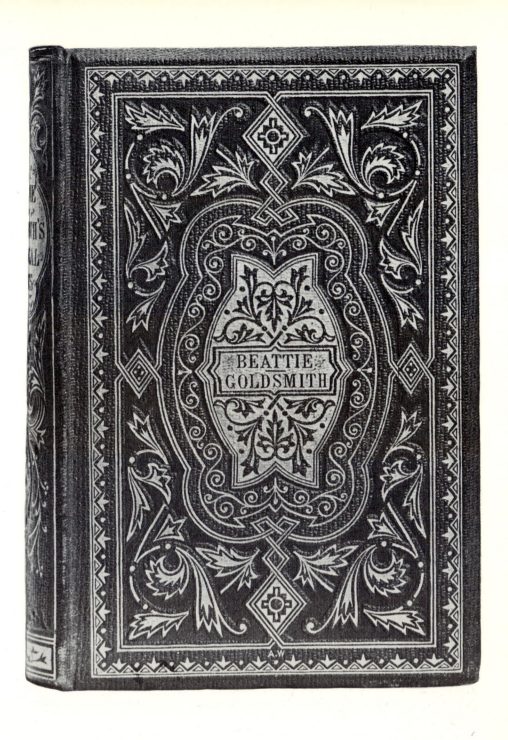

Poetical Works of Beattie & Goldsmith
W. P. Nimmo, Edinburgh, n.d.
  (inscribed 1867)
172 × 109 mm

Red cloth blocked in gold and blind
on front and spine, in blind on back,
bevelled boards. Signed A.W.
Collection Fianach Lawry

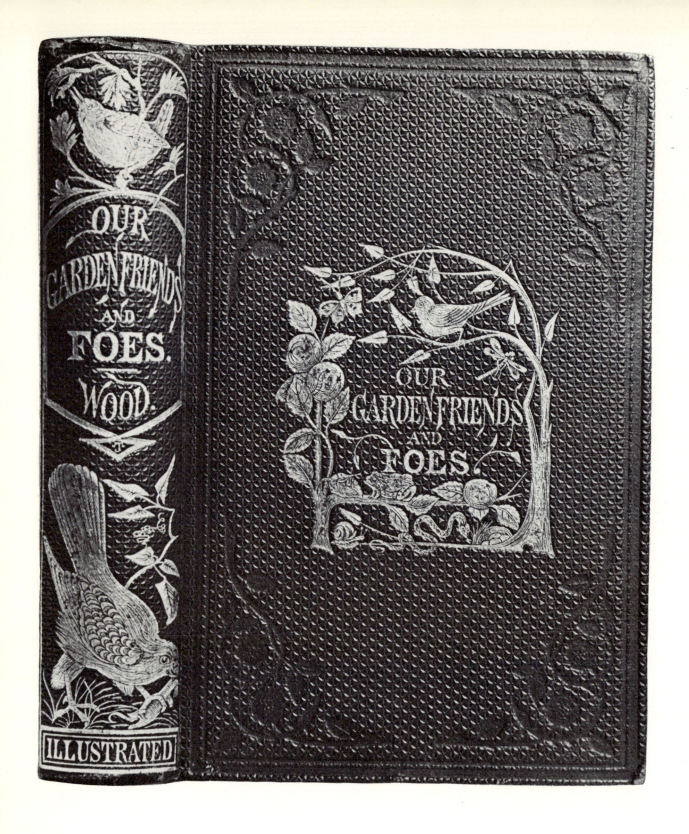

Our Garden Friends and Foes
Rev. J. G. Wood
Routledge, 1864
194 × 127 mm

Green honeycomb cloth blocked in gold and blind on front, in gold on spine, and blind on back. Signed (T.J.?) on spine.
Collection Fianach Lawry

Little Songs for Me to Sing
Ill. J. E. Millais
Cassell, Petter & Galpin, n.d.
(*c.*1865)
175 × 165 mm

Green cloth blocked in gold on front
and spine, bevelled boards
Collection Fianach Lawry

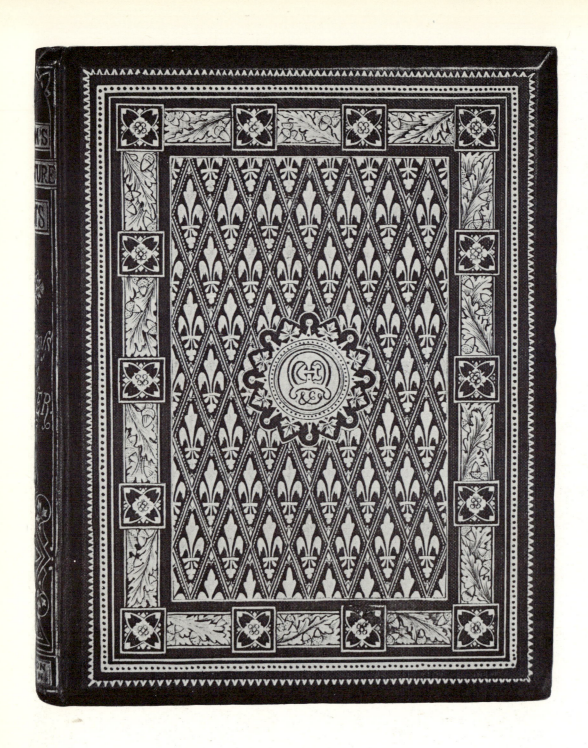

A Selection from the work of Frederick Locker
Ill. R. Doyle
Moxon, 1865
170 × 125 mm

Brown cloth blocked in gold on front
and spine, in blind on back, bevelled
boards.
  The cover block was also used for
Selections from Tennyson, in the same
year, and has been attributed to John
Leighton, although Leighton rarely
used repeating patterns.
Collection Fianach Lawry

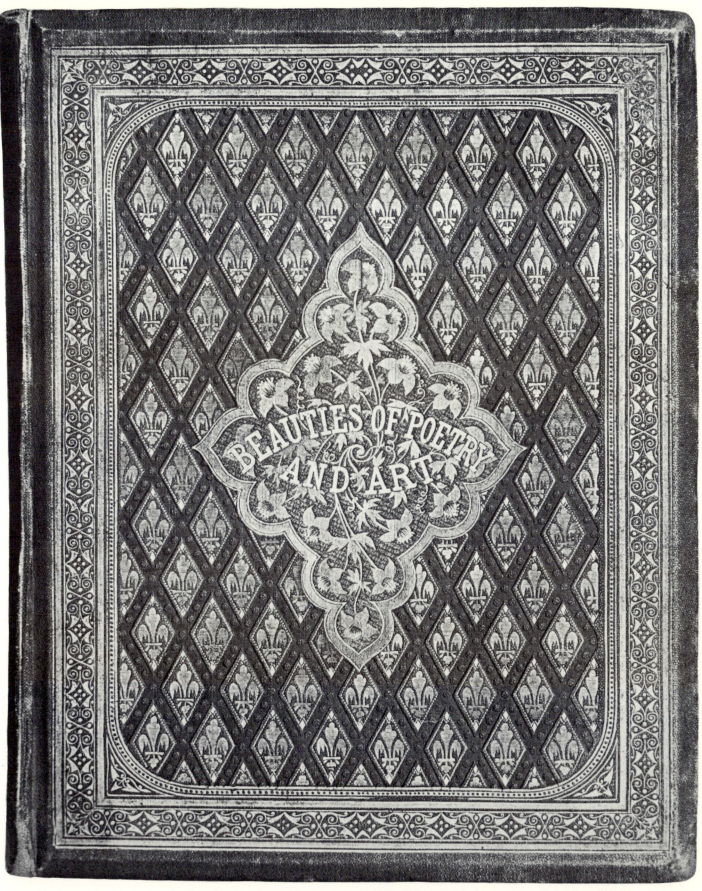

Beauties of Poetry and Art
With colour plates by Edmund Evans
Ward, Lock & Tyler, n.d. (*c.* 1865)
242 × 177 mm

The Duc d'Orléans, brother of
Louis XIII, owned a manuscript
Passionale, bound *c.*1630 in morocco
with a closely similar diaper of dotted
lines enclosing fleur-de-lys, illustrated
on plate 62 of Sotheby's Catalogue of
the Sale of Major Abbey's books on
21–23 June 1965.

Blue cloth with cut-out red paper
onlay blocked in gold and blind on
front, blocked in gold and blind only
on back, in gold on spine, bevelled
boards. Another repeating pattern
using the fleur-de-lis, with a subtle
use of blind stamping which raises
the diamond shapes bearing the
fleur-de-lis; an altogether more
dignified and harmonious design than
that on the facing page.

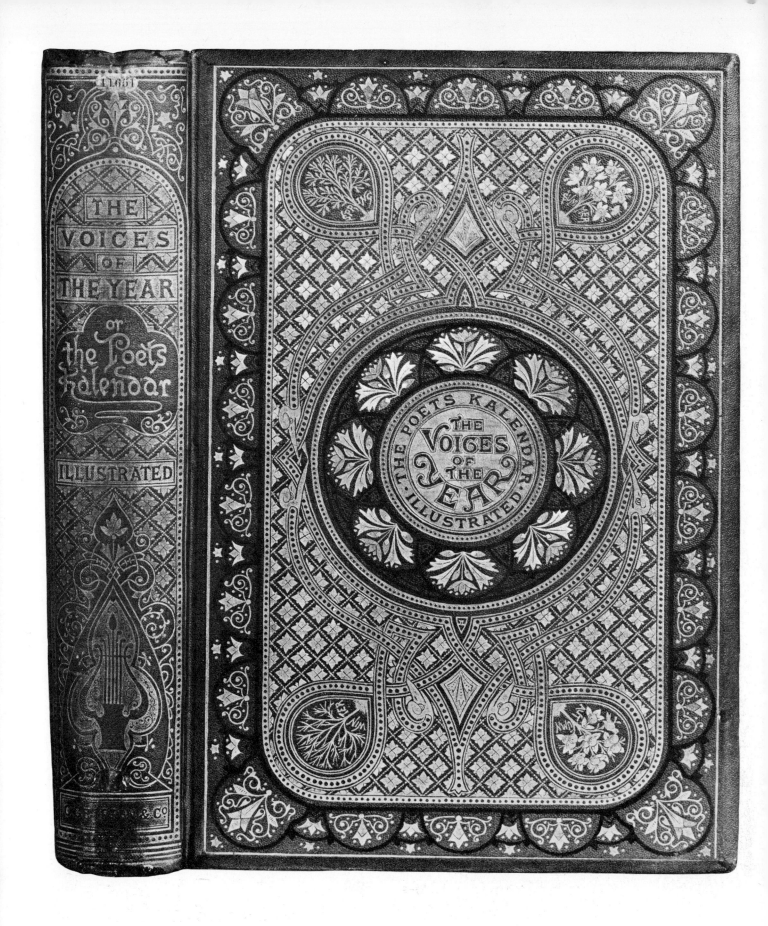

The Voices of the Year, or, *The Poet's Kalendar*
Charles Griffin, 1865
252 × 158 mm

Blue cloth blocked in gold and black
(identical on front and back) on front,
back and spine. Signed JL. Bevelled
boards.
British Museum

Gems of English Art
Routledge, 1869
262 × 190 mm

Purple cloth, with paper, coloured in purple, red, blue, and green, laid over whole of front cover, blocked in gold. Spine blocked in gold only, back blocked in gold and blind, bevelled boards.

This is a remarkably successful Victorian version, by mass-production methods, of a costly hand-tooled polychrome leather binding. The colours on the paper cover must have been stencilled.
Collection Fianach Lawry

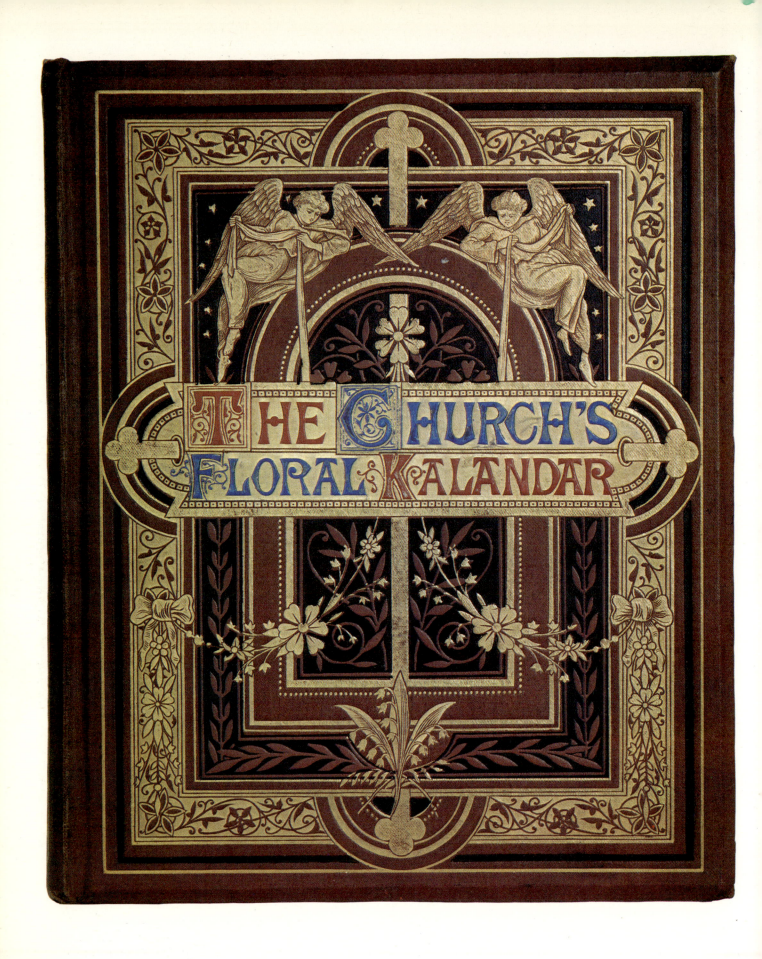

The Church's Floral Kalandar
Illuminated and chromolithographed
  by W. R. Tymms
Day & Son, n.d. (*c.* 1869)
245 × 190 mm

Brown cloth with blue and red
pigment, possibly stencilled onto the
cloth, the whole blocked in gold and
back. Some colouring has been added
after the gold blocking. Spine blocked
in gold only, back in blind, bevelled
boards. Label: Bound by Leighton
Son & Hodge.
Collection Fianach Lawry

The Ancestral Homes of Britain
F. O. Morris, ill. A. F. Lydon
Bell & Daldy, 1868
282 × 222 mm

Brown cloth blocked in gold and blind on front and spine, in blind on back, bevelled boards. Unsigned, probably by John Leighton, who designed the covers of the complete work, *Picturesque Views of Seats etc.* of which this is part (see page 115). Bound by Burn.

Rambles in the Rhine Provinces
John P. Seddon, ill. with chromolithographs, photographs and wood-
  engravings
Murray, 1868
280 × 215 mm

Blue cloth blocked in gold, black and
blind on front, in gold and black on
spine, and in blind on back.
  A riotous and intriguing design
inspired by 'artistic printing', which
bears no relation to the chaste
Chiswick Press typography of the
inside.

Poems of Thomas Hood
Ill. B. Foster
E. Moxon, 1871
288 × 216 mm

Mauve cloth blocked in gold on front
and spine, in gold and blind on back.
Leighton Son & Hodge. Art Deco?
or 'artistic printing' inspired.
British Museum

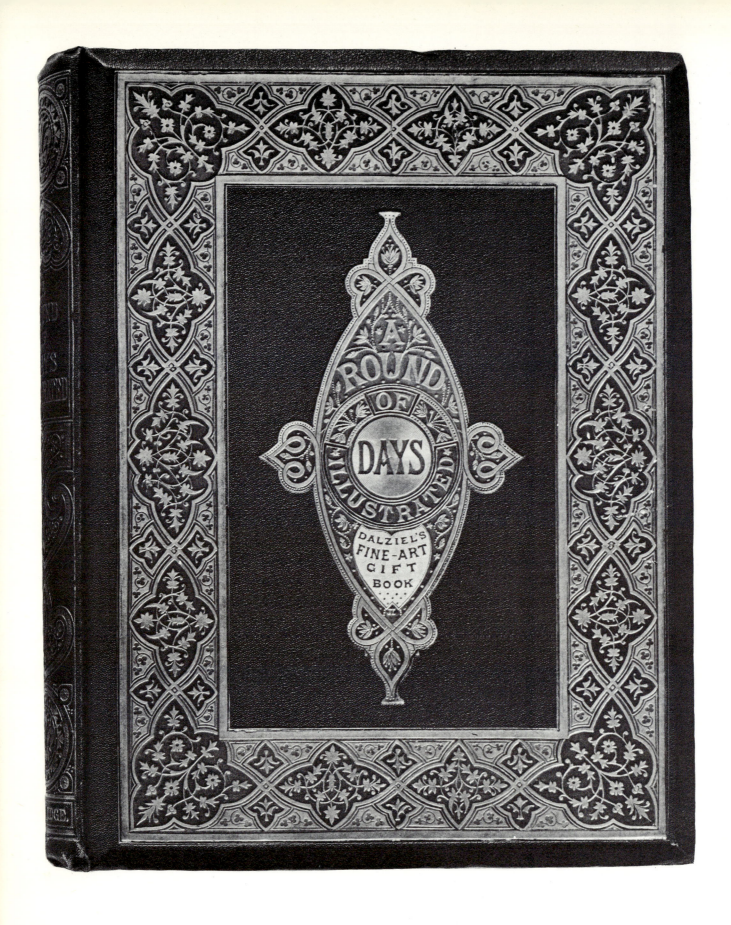

A Round of Days
A Dalziel Fine-Art Gift Book
Routledge, 1866
264 × 202 mm

Green sand-grained cloth with red
and blue cut-out paper onlays
blocked in gold, bevelled boards.
Signed JL.
  This impressive design is reproduced
in colour in Quayle's *The Collector's
Book of Books*

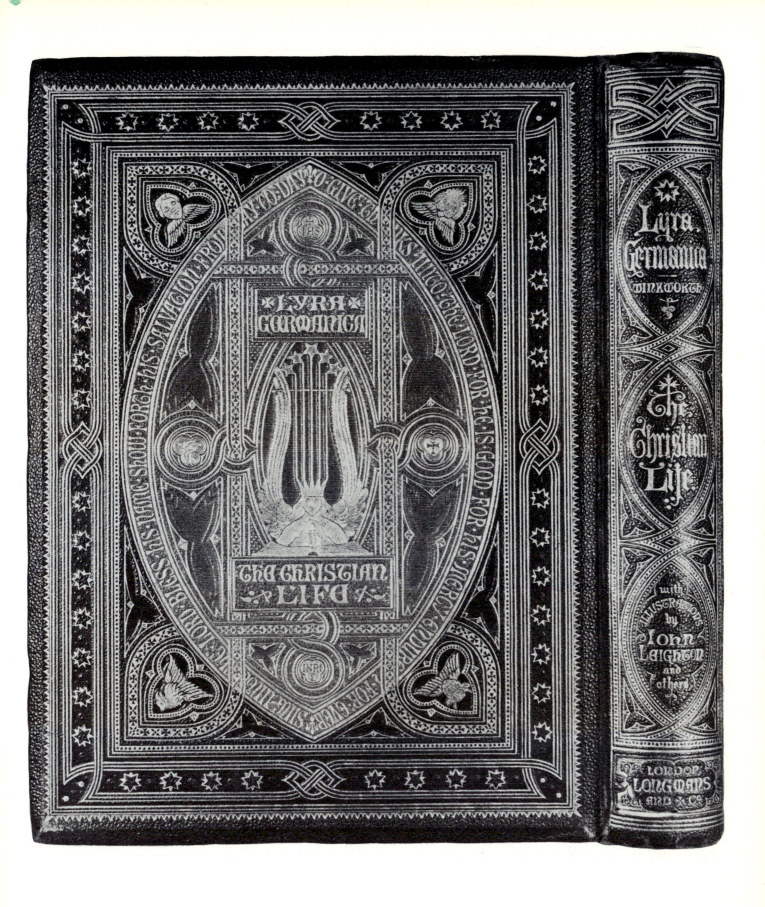

Lyra Germanica
C. Winkworth, ill. John Leighton
Longman, 1868
235 × 170 mm

Green morocco-grained cloth with
crimson cloth mandorla onlay,
blocked in gold on sides, identical
design on front and back, and on
spine, bevelled boards. Signed J.L.
Bound by Edmonds & Remnants.

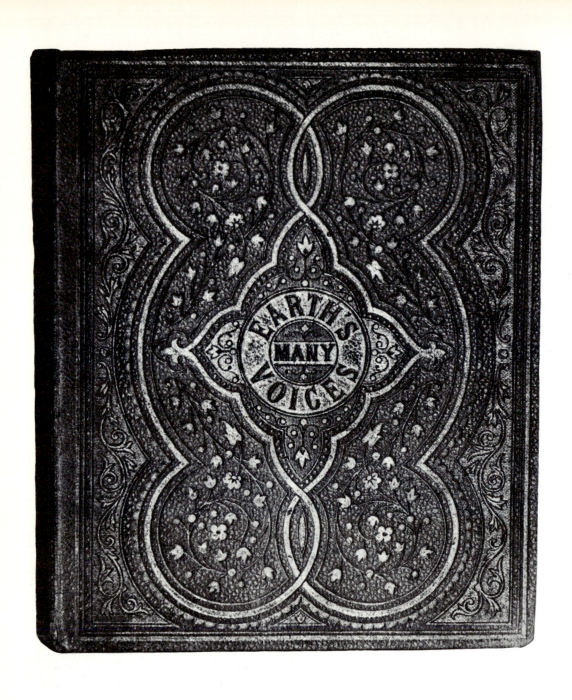

Earth's Many Voices
S.P.C.K., n.d. (*c.*1870)
160 × 125 mm

Orange cloth blocked in gold on
front and spine, in blind on back.
Collection Fianach Lawry

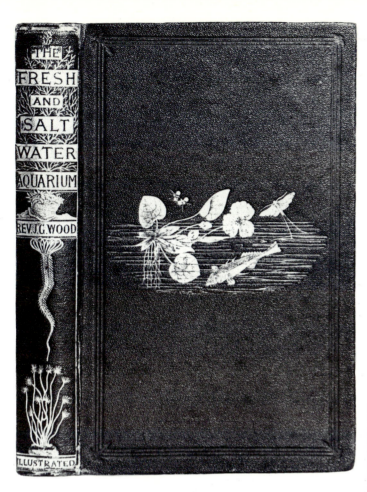

The Fresh and Salt-Water Aquarium
Rev. J. G. Wood
Routledge, 1868
170 × 105 mm

Blue morocco-grained cloth blocked
in gold and blind on front, in gold on
spine. Bound by W. Bone & Son.
Collection Fianach Lawry

Country Walks of a Naturalist with his
Children
Rev. W. Houghton
Groombridge, 1869
187 × 123 mm

Blue cloth blocked in gold and black
on front and spine.

Enoch Arden
A. Tennyson, ill. Arthur Hughes
Moxon, 1866
225 × 171 mm

Blue morocco-grained cloth blocked in gold on front, back and spine, bevelled boards. Design possibly by Arthur Hughes, but more in the style of John Leighton.

Beautiful Butterflies
Groombridge, 1871
187 × 123 mm

Blue cloth blocked in gold and black
on front and spine.

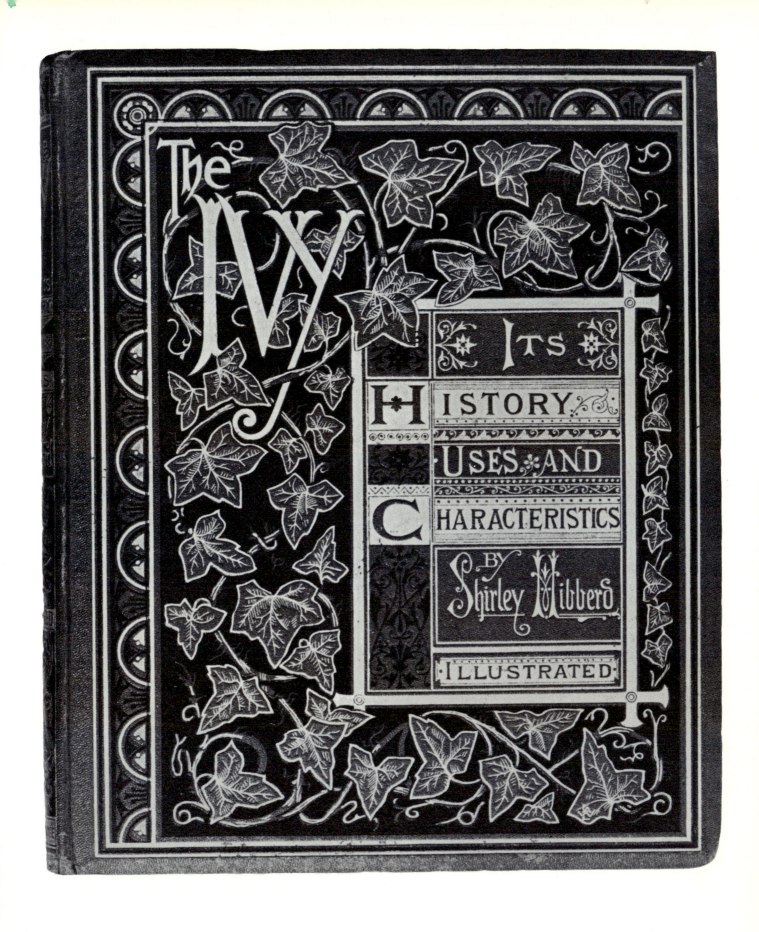

The Ivy
Shirley Hibberd
Groombridge, 1872
216 × 167 mm

Green cloth blocked in gold and black on front and spine, bevelled boards.

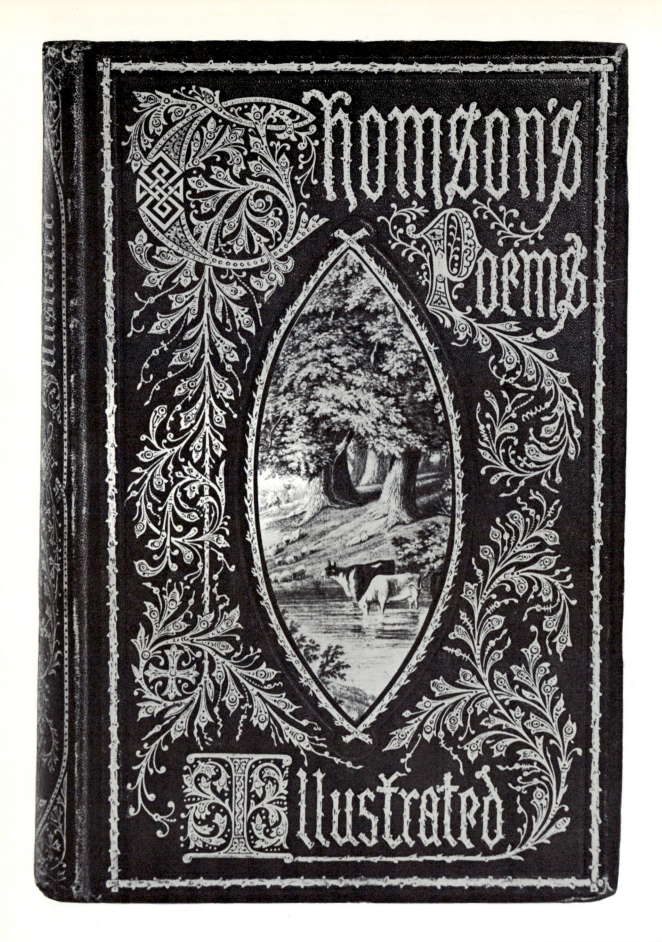

The Poetical Works of James Thomson
Nimmo, Edinburgh, 1869
222 × 140 mm

Blue fine-grained cloth blocked in
blind and gold, with mandorla
colour-printed paper onlay by Kronheim (because six Kronheim colour
prints in book) on front, bevelled
boards.
Collection Fianach Lawry

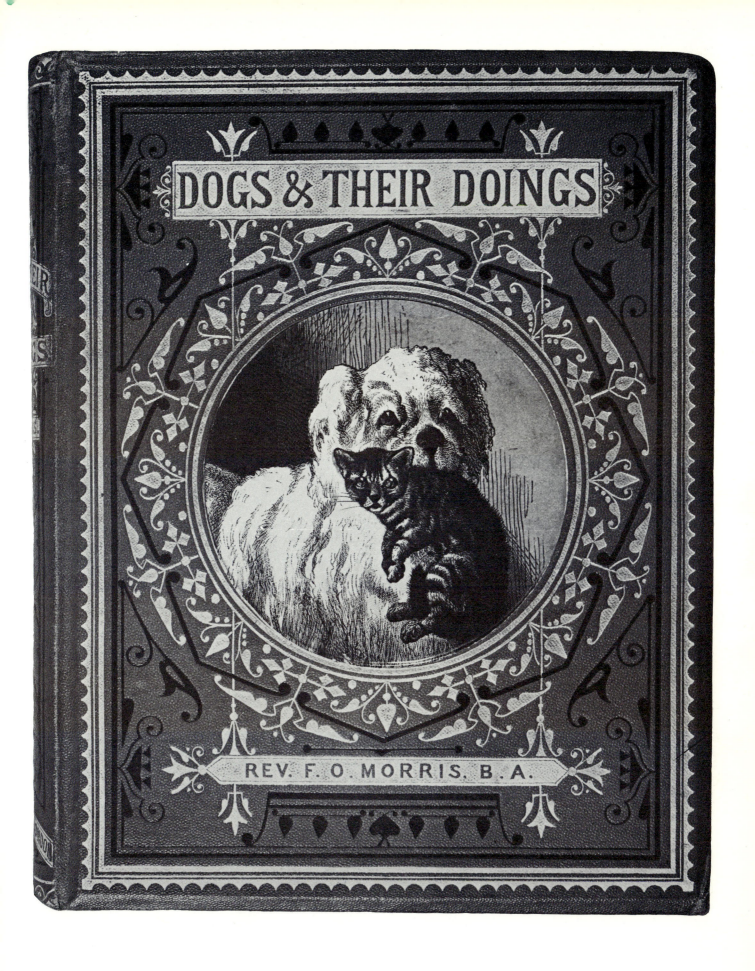

Dogs and their Doings
Rev. F. O. Morris
S. W. Partridge, n.d. (*c.*1870)
215 × 165 mm

Brown cloth blocked in gold and black, with colour-printed paper onlay in sunk circular panel, bevelled boards.

Pastor C. H. Spurgeon, His Life &
Work
George J. Stevenson
Passmore & Alabaster, 1877
219 × 140 mm

Green cloth blocked in gold and
black with oval photograph pasted
down.
Collection R. de Beaumont

The Welcome Hour
The Book Society, 1877
222 × 158 mm

Brown cloth blocked in gold and black with colour printed paper onlay.

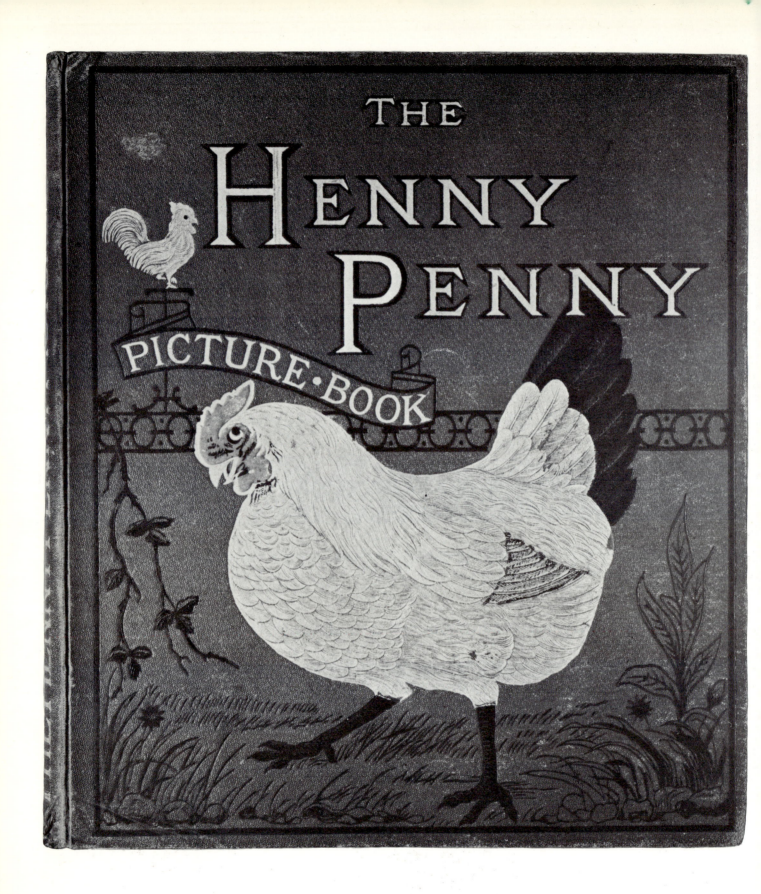

The Henny Penny Picture Book
Routledge, n.d. (c.1870)
273 × 228 mm

Green cloth blocked in gold and
black, with cut-out red paper onlay.

Beauty and the Beast
Ill. E.V.B.
Sampson Low, n.d. (*c.*1876)
266 × 198 mm

Black cloth with four circular and one oblong white paper onlays, printed and blocked in gold. Spine blocked in gold only, back in blind, bevelled boards. Label: Bound by Burn & Co.

This extraordinary un-Victorian design bears no apparent relation to E.V.B's illustrations in the book, which include ten plates printed in colours by Leighton Brothers, and numerous small wood engravings in the style of Dicky Doyle. any one of which could have been easily used on the cover.
Collection D. Parkinson

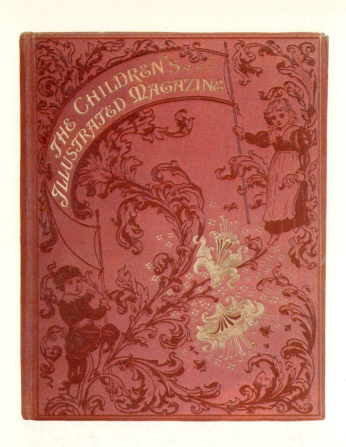

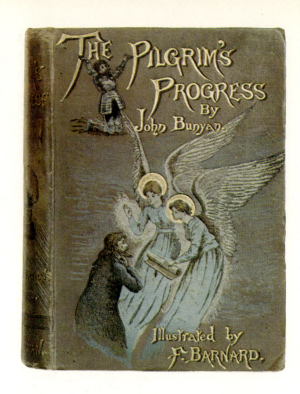

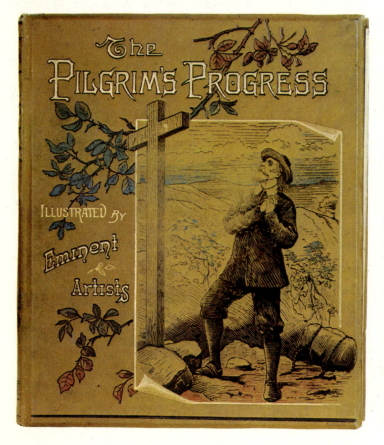

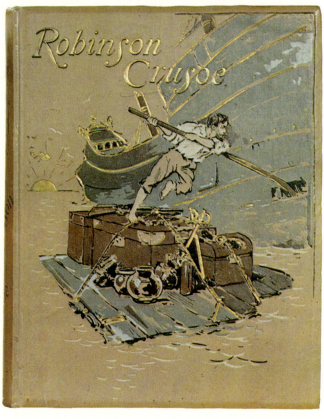

The Children's Illustrated Magazine
Seeley & Co., 1888
228 × 173 mm

Red cloth blocked in gold and red on front, in gold only on spine. An unsigned design far in advance of the debased styles of its period and perhaps influenced by A. H. Mackmurdo, whose *Wren's City Churches* was published in 1883.

The Pilgrim's Progress
John Bunyan
Ill. Fred Barnard and others
Alexander Strahan, 1889
200 × 135 mm

Grey cloth blocked in gold, yellow, blue, black and white.

The Pilgrim's Progress
John Bunyan
Ill. F. Barnard and others
S. W. Partridge, n.d. (Prize label dated 1895)
245 × 200 mm

Yellow cloth blocked in gold, red, blue, green and black, bevelled edges.

Robinson Crusoe
D. Defoe
Ernest Nister, n.d. (c.1900?)
236 × 178 mm

Puce cloth blocked in gold, blue, brown, black and white.

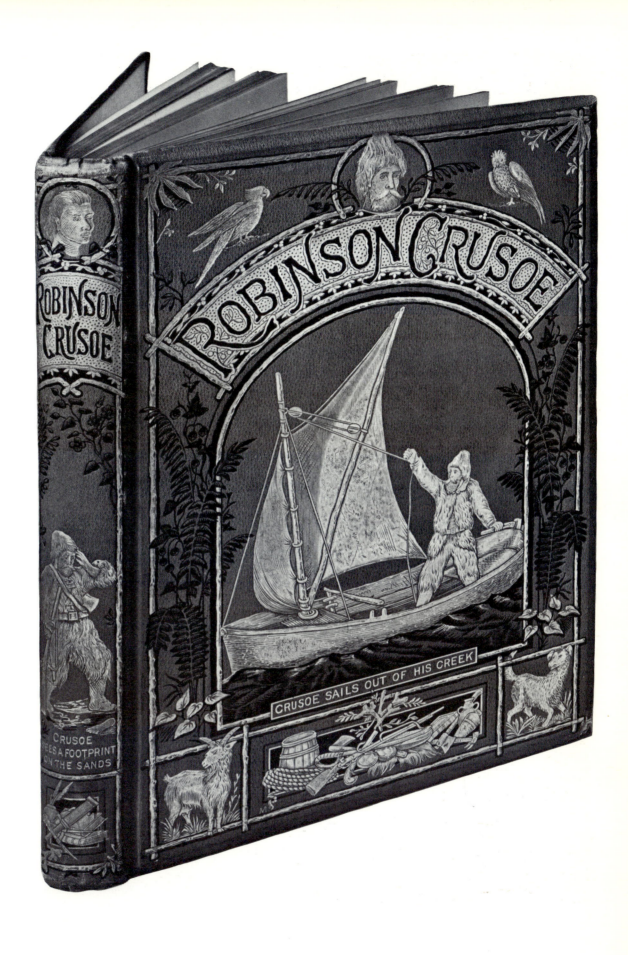

Robinson Crusoe
D. Defoe
Cassell, Petter & Galpin n.d. (*c.*1876)
273 × 190 mm

Brown cloth blocked in gold and black on front and spine, bevelled boards. Signed M (for Macquoid?).

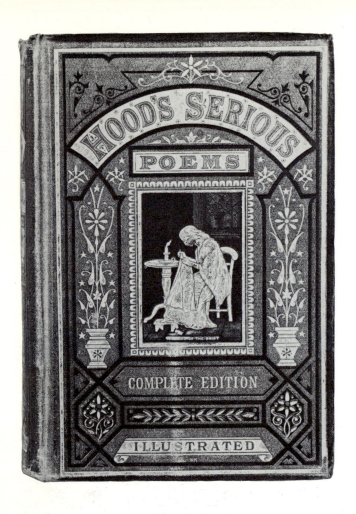

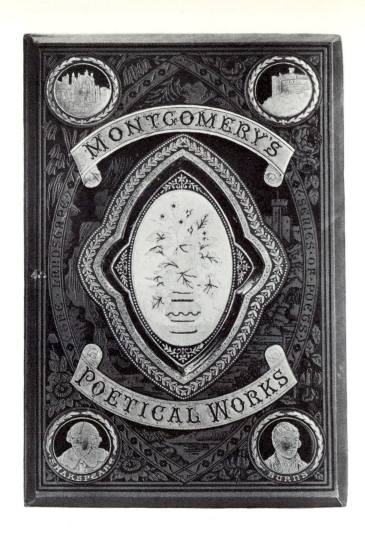

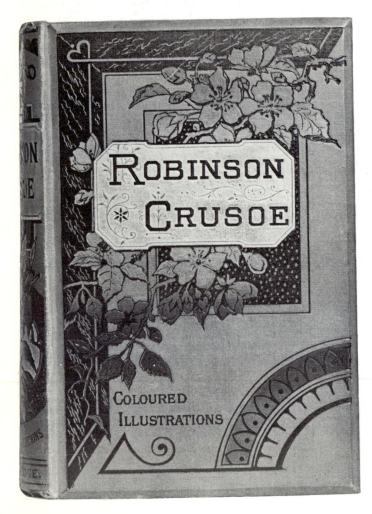

Hood's Serious Poems
Moxon, 1876
184 × 130 mm

Red sand-grained cloth blocked in gold and black on front and spine, bevelled boards. Signed WK.
Collection Jeff Clements

Montgomery's Poetical Works
Gall & Inglis, n.d. (c.1880)
195 × 138 mm

Brown ribbed cloth blocked in gold, blue, and black, with varnished paper cut-out centrepiece blocked in gold and brown ink in recessed panel.
Collection Jeff Clements

Robinson Crusoe
D. Defoe
Routledge, n.d. (c 1880?)
187 × 120 mm

Fawn cloth blocked in gold and black and printed in split-duct colours in red, yellow, and green on front and spine.

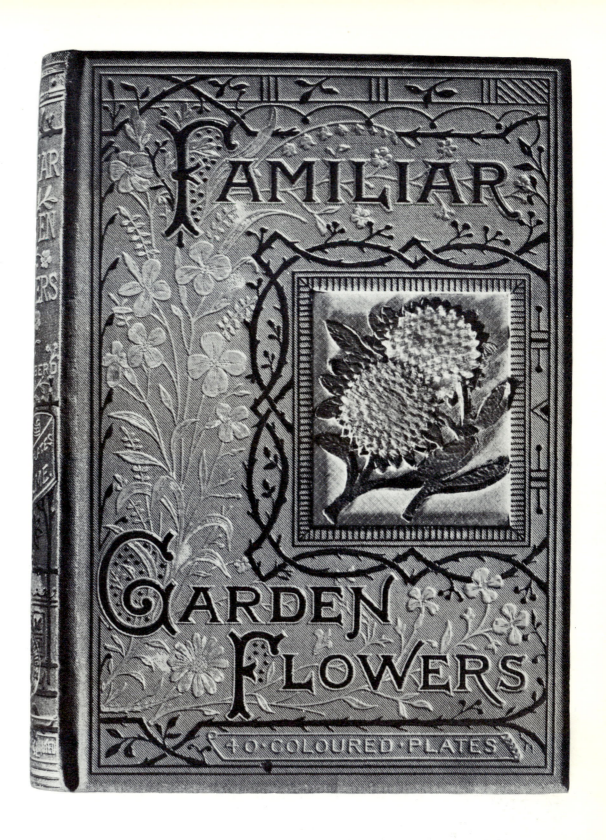

Familiar Garden Flowers
Shirley Hibberd
Cassell, n.d. (*c.*1880)
197 × 126 mm

Pale blue diagonal-ribbed cloth, heavily embossed and blocked in gold and black, with rectangular sunk cut-out panel, containing cut-out flowers in green leather with crimson and mauve silk onlays. Each of the five volumes in the series had a different flower in the cut-out panel.

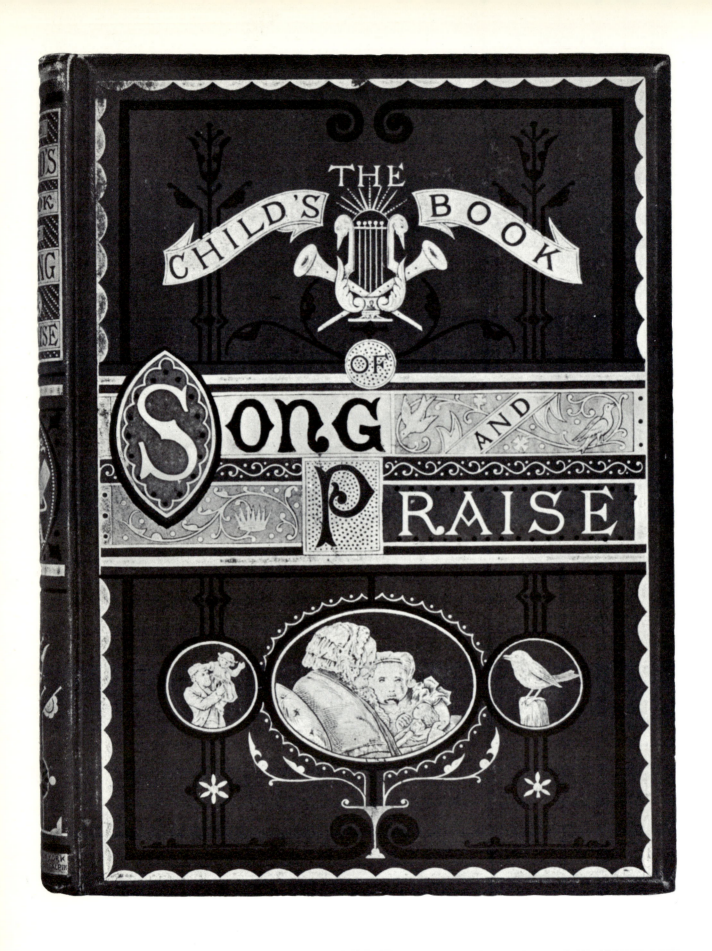

The Child's Book of Song and Praise
Cassell, Petter & Galpin, n.d.
  (*c*.1880?)
263 × 187 mm

Green cloth with two red leather
onlays, blocked in gold and black on
front and spine, bevelled boards.

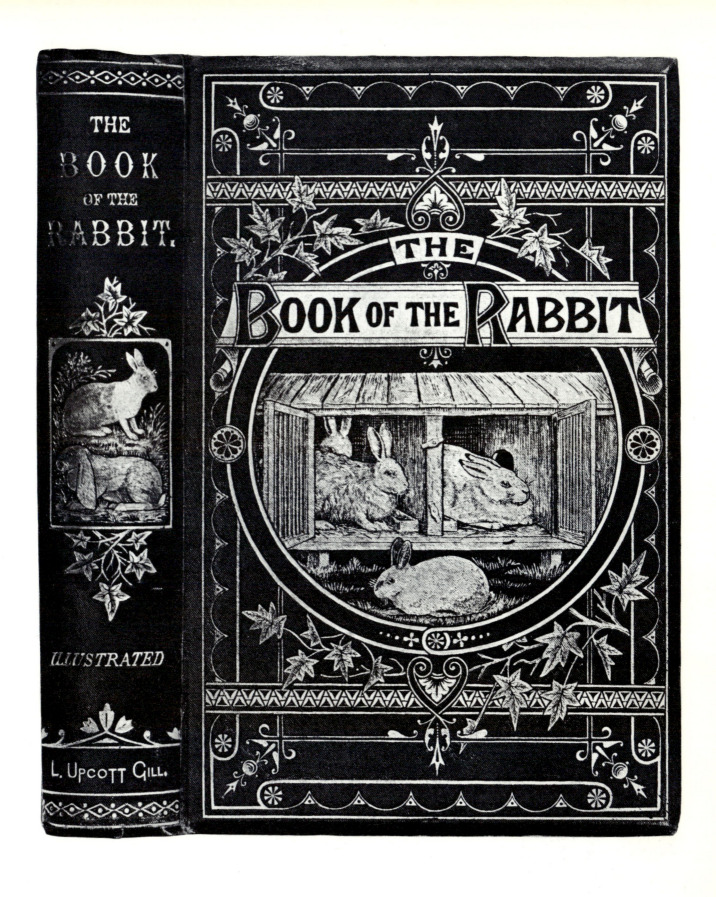

The Book of the Rabbit
Ed. Leonard U. Gill
The 'Bazaar' Office, 1881
203 × 127 mm

Green cloth blocked in gold on front
and spine, in blind on back.
Collection Fianach Lawry

Lady Brassey's Three Voyages in the
Sunbeam
1889
317 × 222 mm

Pink cloth blocked in green, blue-
grey, and black.

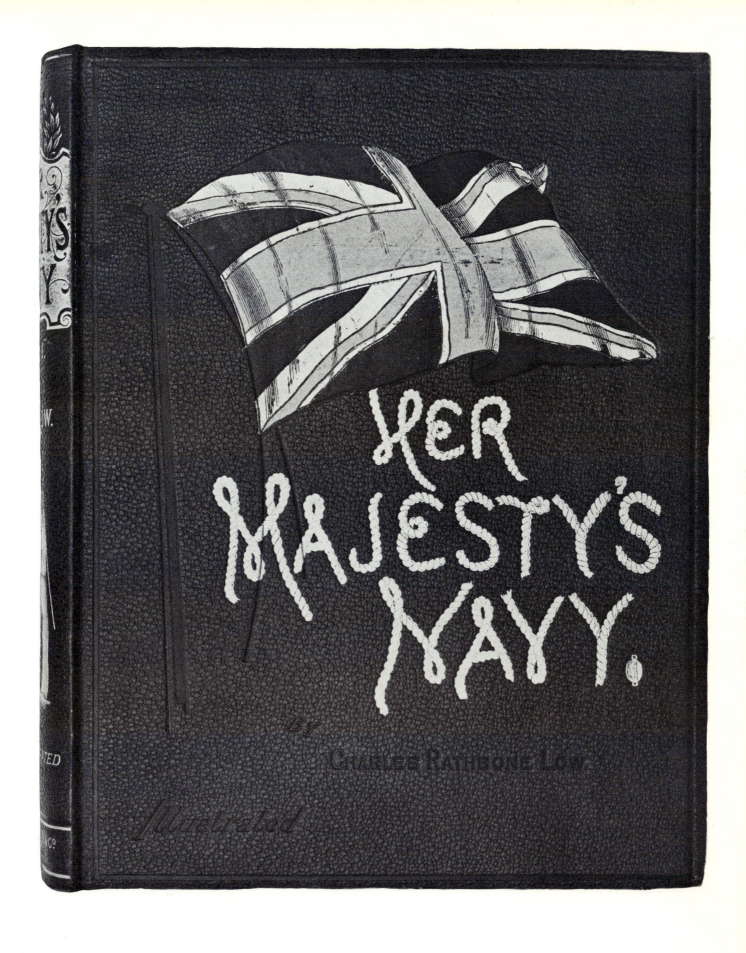

Her Majesty's Navy
C. R. Low, ill. W. Christian Symons
 and W. Fred Mitchell
J. S. Virtue, n.d. (*c.*1892)
286 × 216 mm

Blue pebbled cloth blocked in gold,
black, white, red, and blind.

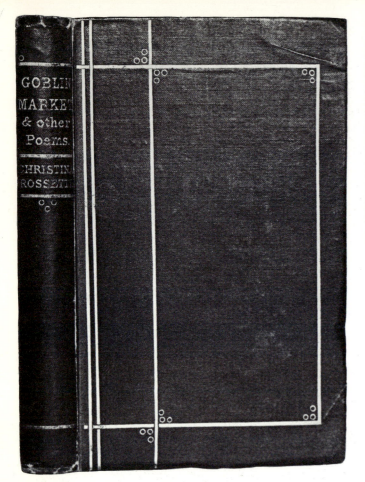

Goblin Market
C. Rossetti
Macmillan, 1865
175 × 106 mm

Blue cloth blocked in gold on front
and spine, blind on back. Designed
by D. G. Rossetti, slightly modified
from the design which originally
appeared on the first edition, 1862.
Collection Fianach Lawry

The Prince's Progress
C. Rossetti
Macmillan, 1866
178 × 106 mm

Green cloth blocked in gold on front
and spine. Designed by D. G. Rossetti.

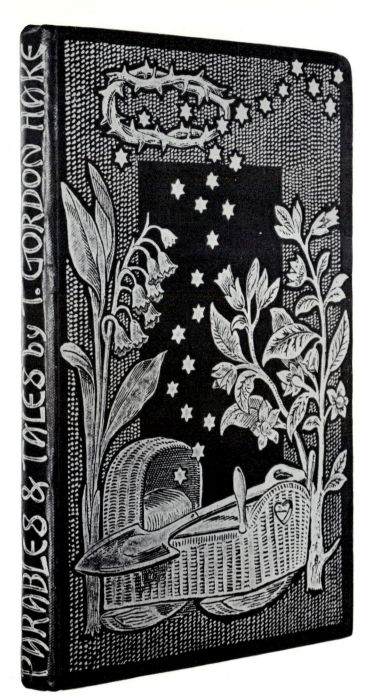

Parables & Tales
T. Gordon Hake, ill. Arthur Hughes
Chapman & Hall, 1872
190 × 127 mm

Blue cloth blocked in gold on front
and spine. Designed by D. G.
Rossetti.
Collection R. de Beaumont

Sunflowers: A Book of Verses
H. Gardner
H. S. King, 1876
180 × 115 mm

Blue-green cloth blocked in gold on
front, back, and spine.
Collection R. de Beaumont

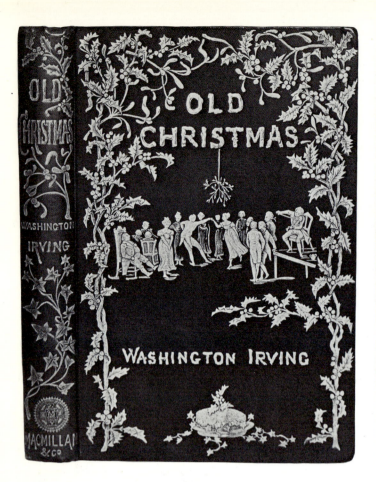

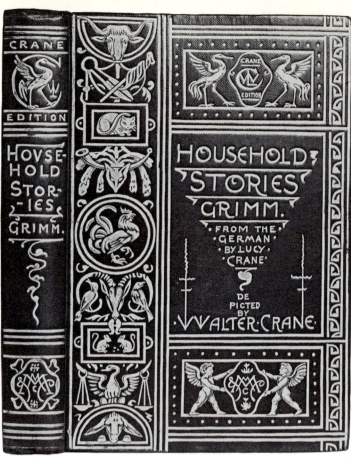

Old Christmas
Washington Irving
Macmillan, 1886
187 × 120 mm

Dark blue cloth blocked in gold on
front and spine.

Household Stories, from Grimm
Ill. Walter Crane
Macmillan, 1893
187 × 122 mm

Dark blue cloth blocked in gold on
front and spine, designed by Walter
Crane.

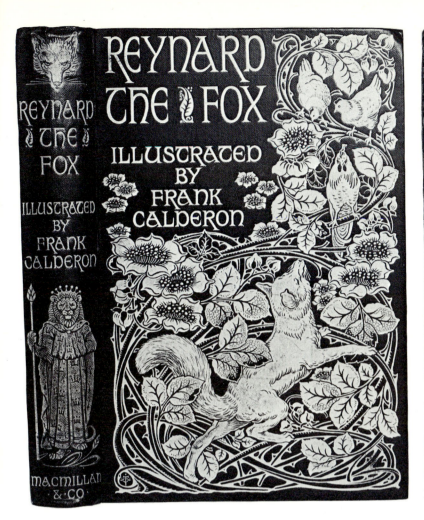

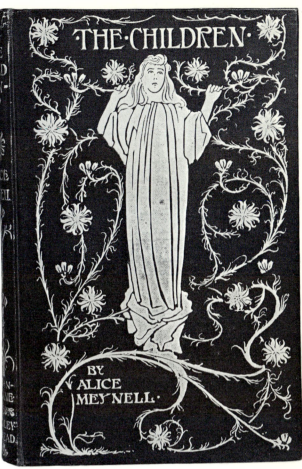

Reynard the Fox
Ill. W. Frank Calderon
Macmillan, 1895
186 × 122 mm

Dark blue cloth blocked in gold on
front and spine. Designed by A. A.
Turbayne

The Children
Alice Meynell
John Lane, 1897
178 × 112 mm

Blue cloth blocked in gold on front
and spine. Perhaps designed by
Charles Robinson.

Her Ladyship's Elephant
D. D. Wells
Heinemann, 1898
195 × 127 mm

Buff canvas blocked in black, grey, and yellow on front and spine, in black on back. From a design by William Nicholson.

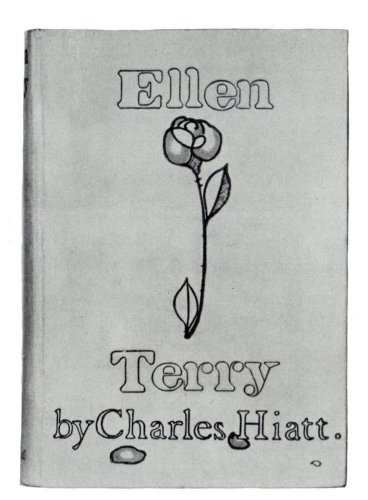

Ellen Terry
Charles Hiatt
George Bell, 1898
194 × 128

White cloth blocked in gold, green
and pink on front, spine, and back
(different designs on front and back)
after a design by E. Gordon Craig.

Henry Irving
Charles Hiatt
George Bell, 1899
200 × 128 mm

Buff cloth blocked in gold, black,
green, and grey, on front and spine,
after a design by E. Gordon Craig.

Life's Roses
Ernest Nister, n.d. (inscribed 1898)
230 × 164 mm

Blue cloth blocked in gold, green,
red, and blue-grey, on front and
spine.

Index

Bold figures refer to illustrations